Prophetic Faith

Exploring Social Justice Advocacy as a Congregation

An Adult Study for Congregations

by Trish Towle Greeves

Participant Book

Prophetic Faith

Participant Book

Contents

Introduction

Welcome to *Prophetic Faith,* an opportunity for you to join with others in your local community to discover, think about, and explore the relationship between your Christian faith, social justice, and the public role of the church. This study invites you to ask how we, as individuals and as congregations, can respond to the biblical call for social justice in ways that are faithful to our vocation as followers of Jesus Christ and yet respect the pluralistic democracy in which we live and comply with the separation of church and state mandated by the U.S. Constitution.

Although the call for God's people to advocate on behalf of "the least of these" (Mt 25:40) is a clear mandate of our Christian faith, many churches and their members resist this responsibility, focusing instead exclusively on "spiritual" issues of belief, forgiveness, salvation, and eternal life to the exclusion of more controversial social issues, because congregations don't want to risk causing dissention among their members. The consequence of this avoidance is a diminished gospel in a world where too many people are not receiving the daily bread for which Jesus taught us to pray.

This course seeks to overcome resistance to social justice ministry by providing a structure and a safe, mutually respectful space where people can examine their beliefs about the role of faith in the public sphere and discuss these ideas with one another. Ideally, the people who participate in the study with you will reflect differing backgrounds and hold a variety of opinions so that all of you can learn from each other through open-minded listening and honest sharing of ideas.

These are deeply divided times. Sadly, two of the things about which people are most divided are religion, which calls us to live in peace with our brothers and sisters, and politics and governance, the process through which we direct our common life together in a way that brings about "liberty and justice for all." We may falsely assume that the church must choose between a "spiritual" and a "worldly" focus and that one detracts from the other. To the contrary, the voice of a spiritually grounded, faith-informed church is desperately needed in today's polarized world.

The cultural divide in our country is exacerbated by the tendency for many of us to read and listen selectively, seeking sources of information that simply confirm what we already believe. We keep company with people who think like we do, and we find it easy to stereotype others, comparing our best to their worst and feeling smug about it. Some of us look down upon one another as "Bible-thumping fundamentalists" or "lukewarm, culturally accommodating liberals." One purpose of this study is to provide incentives and opportunities for your study group to reach beyond self-imposed barriers and stereotypes and, in so doing, to grow in faith, understanding, and mutual affection.

Overview of Prophetic Faith

The material in this Participant Book is intended to lay the groundwork for the activities and discussions outlined in the companion resource, *Leader Guide for Prophetic Faith: Exploring Social Justice Advocacy as a Congregation*. You will get the most out of these discussions if you have read and digested the material in each chapter of the Participant Book prior to the group study session. The topics and goals for each session are the following:

Session 1: Private Faith and Public Practice

In this first session, you and other group members will develop a sense of community for respectful listening and honest sharing, explore the biblical understanding of justice as the way in which faith and politics come together for Christians, and learn and use a model for holistic faith and practice. Read this session before the first meeting of the group.

Session 2: The Church's Prophetic Heritage

You and other participants will examine how the church's advocacy of social justice is rooted in the teaching of the Old Testament prophets and the ministry of Jesus. You will learn to distinguish between acts of mercy and charity to alleviate immediate needs and social justice ministry that seeks to reduce the structural causes for those needs. And you will begin to explore the call to follow Jesus as one that takes you into the world as speakers of truth to power and agents of positive change.

Session 3: Perspective Makes a Difference

This session will help you and other participants recognize that each of us has limited experience in the world. You will examine the concept of social location as a means for expanding your awareness and develop listening skills in order to expand your experience base.

Session 4: Sowing Seeds for Justice

This session marks the midpoint of your study. With other participants, you will explore how social justice consciousness is nurtured and resisted and consider the time this process takes. The group will generate ideas for actively nurturing a conscience for social justice in your congregation.

Session 5: God and Emperor: Discerning the Dividing Line

You will begin to discern and clarify both legal dividing lines and the areas of cultural overlap between church and state, in anticipation of your congregation's engagement with political and legal processes as you pursue social justice ministry.

Session 6: Beyond Avoidance: Healthy Conflict Is Possible

Conflict is inevitable in human relationships. In this session you will learn to identify healthy and unhealthy conflict behaviors and practice communicating in a conflicted situation.

Session 7: Strengthening Our Congregation's Public Witness

You will identify the elements for effective social justice ministry in the church and practice a group process for consensus planning and decision-making, resulting in some next steps for your congregation's social justice ministry.

Your Part in the Process

As you read and when you meet with your study group, take some risks in your thinking and sharing. As always, the more you can prepare for the group sessions, the more you will have to offer and gain. The Personal Reflection questions embedded throughout the reading will help you do this. And keep in mind that what you share from these reflections is always your decision alone. Enjoy the process and the relationships you build. Expect both challenge and inspiration. May you grow in love and spirit!

Session One

Private Faith and Public Practice

With both feet planted firmly on love,... take in...
the extravagant dimensions of Christ's love.
- Ephesians 3:18-19, *The Message*

"That was too political," Joe told the pastor as he left the sanctuary after worship one Sunday morning. Joe was referring to the sermon preached that day, and depending on the circumstances and the speaker, such a statement might mean, "I didn't agree with what you said this morning;" or "I'm afraid that may cause some conflict in the congregation;" or, "There was an unacceptable partisan tint to your sermon;" or, "You're supposed to stick with spiritual matters."

The relationship between faith and politics is a perennial struggle, one aspect of which is the question, Should the church be involved in politics or should it limit its concerns to more explicitly "spiritual" matters?

Faith, Politics, and Social Justice Ministry

The very word *politics* conjures loaded connotations for many people. For some, it's the image of a smoke-filled room and associated power brokering, with occasional sleazy deals made on the side. For others, it brings to mind a cut-throat adversarial process carried on via television advertisements, radio talk shows, debates, junk mail, doorbells, telephone calls, emails, and sound bites - all designed to command our loyalty, vote, and money. For many people, politics represents the antithesis of personally accepting into their hearts Jesus Christ who said, "My kingdom is not from this world" (Jn 18:36).

In *Christian Perspectives on Politics,* ethics professor and church pastor J. Philip Wogaman defines politics as "the realm in which we come together and make decisions about the way we structure our common life" (p. 130). Understood this way, political activity is a natural and necessary part of every human relationship and community.

When we speak of *justice* in American society today, we may think of things like courts, judges, prosecutors, and prisons as the means for enforcing law and order. When we hear the word *righteousness,* many of us may focus on matters of personal piety and goodness. In the Bible, however, the Hebrew words most commonly translated as "justice" *(misphat)* and "righteousness" *(sedaqah)* refer to defending the rights of the powerless and society's most vulnerable people so that harmonious relationships are possible. A just society is one where the weak and voiceless are brought to the table to participate and contribute to the life of the community and enjoy its goods and services.

This biblical understanding informs our definition of justice. Achieving *distributive justice* - sharing power and correcting systemic inequalities - always involves a political process. In other words, meaningful religion will inevitably have a political dimension. William Stringfellow, in his book *A Private and Public Faith,* writes, "If religion and politics are separated, then religion and practical life are separated" (p. 22).

The Shema, recited morning and evening by faithful Jews, states: "Hear, O Israel: The Lord is our God, the Lord alone. You shall love the Lord your God with all your heart, and with all your soul, and with all your might" (Deut 6:4-5). Jesus echoed these words in what we call the great commandment, adding "and a second is like it: 'You shall love your neighbor as yourself'" (Mt 22:39, quoting Lev 19:18). Because God is sovereign over every aspect of our lives, Christians are called to seek and embody the will of God in every decision and action including their relationships, their use of resources, and their concern for the welfare of all God's children. This, in a nutshell, is the meaning of Christian discipleship.

Fortunately, we don't live out this high calling as solitary pilgrims dependent only upon our own best thinking and resources. We deepen our understanding and express our love for God as part of the community of God's people. We discern God's word for our world through a rich scriptural and theological heritage shared in worship, study, prayer, fellowship, outreach, service, and mission. Faithful churches nurture this kind of discipleship in the lives of their members, and faithful churches seek to extend God's love and care to neighbors next door and to neighbors around the world.

As we examine the church's vocation to engage in the political affairs of our world, our voice must be shaped not by the cause *de jour* or partisan agendas or cultural trends, but by our Christian faith and tradition. This group study is designed to help local congregations nurture mature, holistic faith among members and discern the implications of that faith for this time and the issues people face. And we do this with humility, always remembering that our vantage point is limited to a particular cultural and historical setting.

We affirm that God is beyond every time, setting, culture, and human effort. In the words of the prophet Isaiah, "For my thoughts are not your thoughts, nor are your ways my ways, says the Lord. For as the heavens are higher than the earth, so are my ways higher than your ways and my thoughts than your thoughts" (Isa 55:8-9).

Human experience, our outlook, and our capacity to fathom the meaning and mysteries of life are finite. Our judgments are tainted by the sins of pride, selfishness, and greed. So, we enter this important discussion with fear and trembling, as the apostle Paul says, trusting that God will be at work in our midst.

Personal Reflection

1. How would you answer the question, "Should the church be involved in social justice ministry?" For example, where would you place yourself on a scale of 1 to 10, with 1 signifying a strong and definite *no* and 10 representing an unqualified *yes*?

2. In general, how comfortable are you talking about social justice ministry? With whom or in what settings is this most likely to happen?

3. What feelings, hopes, or concerns do you have about participating in this study with other members of this church?

Expressing Faith in Different Settings

Sometimes when people talk about their faith, they are referring to their personal belief that certain things are true, such as the belief that Jesus represents the voice of God. At other times they are referring to a deep trust in unseen spiritual realities permeating the universe. In either case, such faith resides both within individuals and within communities formed of likeminded individuals. We can imagine this range of faith settings as a continuum - the *Individual/Communal* scale.

INDIVIDUAL _____ **COMMUNAL**

Individual expression includes our own personal thoughts, spoken words, and actions. *Communal expression* is the collective voice of a church, a synagogue, a mosque or another recognized setting for the practice of organized religion. This scale is not an "either this or that" polarity. A mature

Christian embraces the full spectrum. For example, reading a psalm at home alone is an activity that would be at the *individual* end of the scale, while singing on Sunday morning in the church choir is *communal*. A family Bible study would fall somewhere in the middle.

Another dimension for describing faith expression is a Private/Public continuum.

PRIVATE

PUBLIC

Private faith is practiced in well-defined areas where a common understanding of the faith exists, such as within oneself, the family, or one's local church. At the *public* end of this theoretical scale, we display our faith in the wider society by what we say and do, as in "They will know we are Christians by our love." For example, celebrating the Sacrament of Baptism in a local church on Sunday morning is a private religious act, while joining a protest gathering at the capitol building is a public action. Again, this is not an either-or continuum but a description of the range of settings in which faith is practiced.

Putting the *Individual/Communal* and the *Private/Public* scales together, creates four theoretical *Arenas of Faith Expression*. These are shown in the four quadrants labeled A, B, C, and D on the next page, along with some examples of typical activities:

Private

Individual

One's personal relationship with God; one's inner life; Prayer and meditation; Family faith practices **A**	Local church life and programs; Worship; Christian education; Pastoral care; Rites of passage; Evangelism. **B**
Faith practiced in daily life, work, school and community. One's daily decisions. **C**	**D** Public activity of faith communities; Prophetic witness; Justice ministries

Communal

Public

Quadrant A represents the Individual/ Private arena where a relationship with God is experienced during personal devotions or expressed around the family dinner table. One might think of Jesus' admonition, "Whenever you pray, go into your room and shut the door" (Mt 6:6), or the faith sentiment expressed in hymns such as "Just a Closer Walk with Thee," or "Precious Lord, Take My Hand." A little further along the continuum, but still largely in Quadrant A, are faith teaching and practices within the family, such as sharing the table blessing or reading Bible stories together.

Quadrant B represents the Communal/Private expression of faith as it is practiced in a religious community. It includes such activities as worship, Christian education, pastoral care, church business meetings, and potluck suppers. Although churches typically refer to worship as "public" worship because it is open to everyone, in this model it is considered communal but private, in the sense that these activities are practiced within the faith community in a designated sacred space. "Blessed Be the Tie that Binds" is a good theme song for the Communal/Private arena (Quadrant B). "They devoted themselves to the apostles' teaching and fellowship, to the breaking of bread and the prayers" (Acts 2:42) describes Quadrant B activity in the early church.

Quadrant C represents the Individual/Public expression of faith through our daily life and decisions at work, at school, and in the community. This arena might include such activities as volunteering, voting, going to a movie, and taking a vacation. The theme song for this quadrant could be "Awake, Awake to Love and Work." Most of the activities of the New Testament parables - farming, giving banquets, and conducting business - describe Quadrant C activities.

The Communal/Public arena, **Quadrant** D, represents the public activity of organized faith communities. This is what we do as a church to affect the way our society functions, such as critiquing social and economic structures, organizing petition drives, sponsoring a food shelf or homeless shelter, and advocating for or against specific legislation. Quadrant D activity encompasses two significant kinds of social engagement: (1) social outreach—that is, acts of mercy and charity, responding to people's immediate survival needs for food, clothing, shelter, and medical care; and (2) social justice ministry, which addresses the root causes of injustice in public structures and institutions and includes activities such as analysis and strategizing, reflection and action, and advocacy. The theme song for Quadrant D could be "The Church of Christ in Every Age" or "Rise Up, O Church of God."

These four quadrants are interdependent and mutually supportive. Each one is essential for mature, authentic expression of Christian faith.

Reflection Question

What activities can you identify from your own life and from the ministry of your faith community that represent each of these arenas? Write several in each quadrant below.

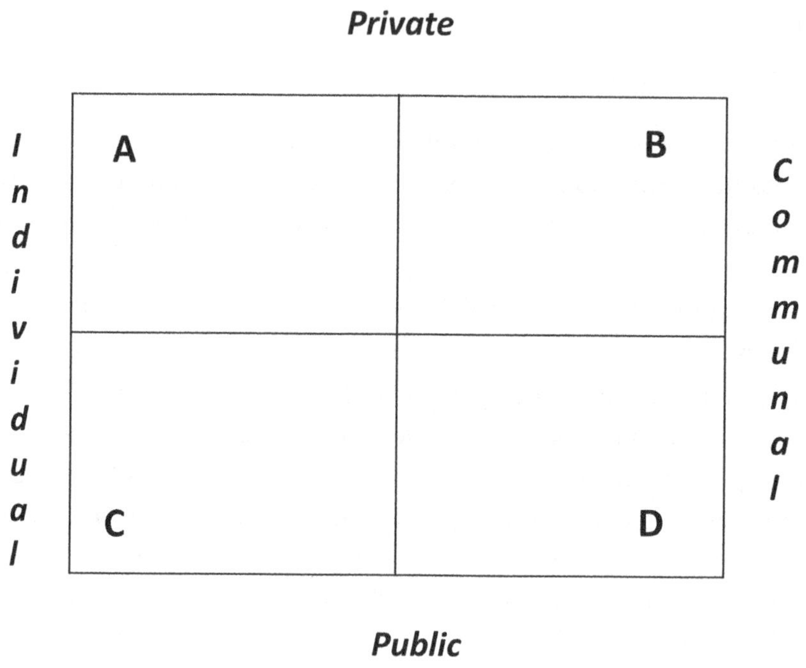

Private

A	B
C	D

(Left axis label: Individual — reading top to bottom: I n d i v i d u a l)

(Right axis label: Communal — reading top to bottom: C o m m u n a l)

Public

Privatized Religion: Resistance to Social Justice Ministry in the Church

"Privatized religion" describes a tendency to divorce faith from everyday life in the world, by emphasizing a personal relationship with God and individual salvation to the exclusion of concrete historical, social, and political implications of one's faith. It often focuses more on life after death than on conditions in this life. Privatized religion is sometimes referred to as a chapel religion for meeting personal and family needs. This kind of religion typically celebrates life passages, provides spiritual comfort and fellowship, encourages acts of mercy and volunteer missions, and promotes evangelism but discourages social justice ministry by the church.

In the book *American Gospel: God, the Founding Fathers, and the Making of a Nation,* author Jon Meacham quotes Jerry Falwell, a former proponent of privatized religion, who spoke these words on March 21,1965, two weeks after Blood Sunday in Selma, Alabama:

> While we are told to "render unto Caesar the things that are Caesar's," in the true interpretation we have very few ties on this earth. We pay our taxes, cast our votes as a responsibility of citizenship, obey the laws of the land, and other things demanded of us by the society in which we live. But at the same time, we are cognizant that our only purpose on this earth is to know Christ and to make him known. Believing the Bible as I do, I would find it impossible to stop preaching the pure saving gospel of Jesus Christ, and begin doing anything else - including fighting Communism, or participating in civil-rights reforms (pp. 198-99).

Falwell's initial preference for privatized religion, demonstrated by the quotation above, evolved considerably as years later he led a national movement bringing evangelical Christians into the thick of American political life. In the meantime, mainline churches, many of which had become politically involved during the 1960s and '70s, retreated into a more privatized stance focused on institutional survival and marketing for church growth.

After the turn of the century, many issues - the wars in Afghanistan and Iraq; the election of Barack Obama, America's first African-American president; the Supreme Court's decision legalizing gay marriage and other polarizing cultural issues; and the extreme divisiveness of the 2016 presidential election - brought diverse religious voices of all persuasions into the political fray. Too often, however, these voices have simply mimicked prevailing partisan ideologies without deep theological reflection and discernment shaping the direction and content of faith-based involvement and the manner in which it is pursued.

Privatized religion focuses on our individual relationship with God, personal morality, works of charity, and the life and worship of the faith community. In other words, privatized religion focuses its concern in quadrants A, B, C, and the social outreach half of D - all of which are important - but skirts around more controversial issues related to social justice ministry. Martin Luther King Jr. criticized this omission in his "Letter from Birmingham Jail": "In the midst of a mighty struggle to rid our nation of racial and economic injustice, I have heard many ministers say: 'Those are social issues, with which the gospel has no real concern.' And I have watched many churches commit themselves to a completely other worldly religion which makes a strange, un-Biblical distinction between body and soul, between the sacred and the secular."

"It's not that the Bible is primarily about our personal relationship with God and oh, by the way, there are a few political implications," states professor and lecturer Marcus Borg. "The Bible is a pervasively political document from beginning to end." Archbishop Desmond Tutu makes a similar assertion in his frequently quoted remark, "I don't know what Bible people are reading when they say faith and politics do not mix." Jesus was not crucified for preaching or practicing privatized religion.

Reflection Questions

1. What do you see as the attraction of privatized religion?

2. Which of the four quadrants do you see most evident in your church?

3. Why might the social justice ministry part of Quadrant D be threatening to many people in churches?

4. What examples of inappropriately "unchristian" political engagement have you observed?

Developing a Holistic Approach

Rather than making an "either this or that" choice between private and public expressions of faith, as maturing Christians:

1. We nurture a rich and sustaining personal relationship with God through individual faith practices and communal worship, study, and fellowship (Quadrants A and B).

2. We live out our faith in every aspect of our lives as we plan, work, play, and relate to God, self, others, and creation (Quadrant C).

3. We are aware and responsive to the needs of others and advocate institutional changes in society when those needs are being systemically violated and neglected (Quadrant D)

The goal of this study is to encourage open-minded thinking and sharing about the appropriate relationship between faith, politics, and justice and to foster respectful listening to all viewpoints. The study's underlying premise is that the church of Jesus Christ, who came to bring good news to the poor and who set his face toward Jerusalem to confront the power structures of his day, must be involved in the affairs of the world. The how, when, who, where, why, substance, and direction of such involvement will be addressed in future sessions.

Session Two
The Church's Prophetic Heritage

Church involvement in the public ministry of social justice predates the beginnings of Christianity by more than 750 years. It is rooted in the words and deeds of the great prophets of Israel who spoke for God during the monarchial period that extended from the ninth to the seventh centuries BCE. The stories of their courage and daring are recorded in the Old Testament books of 1 and 2 Samuel, 1 and 2 Kings, 1 and 2 Chronicles, and the books bearing the names of individual prophets, such as Isaiah, Jeremiah, and Ezekiel.

The reference point for all prophetic critique was the covenant God made with the people of Israel at Mount Sinai and the religious tradition that emerged from that period. That covenant addressed all aspects of life: one's inner thoughts (Quadrant A of the Four Arenas of Faith Expression model), the practices of the worshiping community (Quadrant B), individual behavior (Quadrant C), and communal justice (Quadrant D). With their particular concerns for the well being of the widow, the orphan, and the alien, referring to foreigners or strangers, and their condemnation of the social structures that oppressed them, the prophets specialized in Quadrant D. The challenging witness of the prophets continues today through the social justice ministry of the church.

In this session, we will consider this prophetic tradition and the church's continued call to prophetic witness as we focus on the communal and public activities of the church (Quadrant D).

The Prophetic Call for Justice and Righteousness

As the previous session explored, *justice* and *righteousness* are key words used by the prophets to describe God's vision for human community. The prophet Amos, who lived during the height of Israel's national prosperity, military strength, and territorial security, condemned the extravagant lifestyles of the wealthy, the widespread political corruption, and the increasingly unequal distribution of land. His oft-quoted words represent the essence of the prophetic message to Israel: "Let justice roll down like waters, and righteousness like an ever-flowing stream" (Am 5:24).

The prophets persistently called for a society in which kings ruled justly, the poor were provided for, the strong protected the weak, worship was pure, and religious leaders were authentic. The prophets boldly condemned whoever and whatever contradicted God's expectations for the people of the covenant:

- When King David abused his power by committing adultery with Bathsheba and then engineering her husband's death on the battlefield, the prophet Nathan pronounced God's judgment upon David and his royal household (2 Sam 11-12:15).

- When King Ahab allowed his wife Jezebel to create false charges against Naboth, a neighboring landowner, so that the king could take possession of Naboth's lovely vineyard, the prophet Elijah confronted Ahab on the road saying, "In the place where dogs licked up the blood of Naboth [who had been stoned to death], dogs will also lick up your blood" (1 Kings 21:19).

- When King Jehoshaphat asked for another opinion regarding their planned invasion of Syria, his ally, King Ahab, grudgingly acknowledged there was another prophet around, but he said, "I hate [Micaiah], for he never prophesies anything favorable about me, but only disaster" (1 Kings 22:8).

- When the prophet Amos saw the increasing disparity of wealth between Israel's aristocracy and the peasants who were losing their land, he proclaimed that God would "tear down the winter house as well as the summer house; and the houses of ivory shall perish and the great houses shall come to an end"(Am 3:15).

- When the kings of Judah tried to insure the nation's safety through military alliances instead of through faithfulness to the covenant, the prophet Isaiah predicted that this reliance on power would be turned against them and that the nation would be smashed like a clay pot and left like a lone flagstaff on the top of a mountain (Isa 30:12-17).

- When Isaiah saw that people were just going through the motions of worship - offering the prescribed sacrifices, praying in the temple, and keeping the feasts - but failing to pursue lives of justice and compassion in their dealings with one another (see Isa 1:23), he heard God saying, "Trample my courts no more ... When you stretch out your hands, I will hide my eyes from you; even though you make many prayers, I will not listen" (Isa 1:12,15).

- When rulers put some prophets on the court payroll so that they would parrot the party line, the prophet Jeremiah warned against the reassurances of such false prophets. While the false prophets preached peace and prosperity for Jerusalem, Jeremiah pointed toward approaching calamity that would be God's punishment for Judah's faithlessness and her failure to uphold justice (Jer 7:1-15; 23:16-17).

Speaking Truth to Power

The prophets were social critics who spoke the truth of their deepest religious convictions to those in power, often at great cost to themselves. Most of the prophets were persecuted in some way. They suffered social isolation. Echoing the complaints of Moses before them, they often bemoaned the deafness, blindness, and stubbornness of those who did not listen to them. Some prophets were imprisoned. Amos was expelled from the sanctuary at Bethel and forbidden to preach. Elijah fled to the wilderness to escape the wrath of Jezebel, King Ahab's wife, where he prayed for God to take him out of his misery. Jeremiah, who was tried for treason, lamented the day he was born. Prophets did not win popularity contests with the in-crowd. Their calling was to speak for God.

In contrast to these courageous public stances, privatization of religious faith as described earlier, domesticates the church's voice in society. It robs our world of critical prophetic insights that identify social injustices and provide a check against abuse of power. Issues of justice are usually complicated. Christians may fear offending those in charge or sounding too extreme. The role model the prophets offer can help local congregations overcome the temptation to accommodate the status quo rather than challenge it when God's justice is being thwarted by unjust systems and errant human behaviors.

In the popular mind, prophets have come to be associated with fortunetellers; however, this was not their primary role. Even though prophetic predictions often referred to events anticipated in the immediate future, the intent of such utterances was to foster change in the current behavior of God's people. Old Testament scholar Bernhard W. Anderson in *Understanding the Old Testament* uses this analogy to illustrate the prophetic function: "Just as a doctor's prediction that a patient has only a short time to live makes the patient's present moments more precious and serious, so the prophet's announcement of what God was about to do accented the urgency of the present" (3rd ed., p. 227). Social criticism is not about spreading bad news just to be a negative force in the world. Prophets used the events of their time as interpretive and motivating tools to promote repentance and to effect social change.

Each prophet had his own character, style, and focus. Taken together they provide a rich testimony that faith is private *and* public, individual *and* communal. Their witness reminds us that God's people are called not only to live their own lives with integrity and devotion to God while caring about their neighbor but also to hold leaders accountable for the well being of their subjects and the just exercise of their power. In the language of the Four Arenas model, the great biblical prophets were emphatically and courageously engaged in Quadrant D, public advocacy.

Jesus - The Prophetic Tradition Continues

The prophetic vision of a just and righteous society is not limited to Old Testament accounts. The Gospels present Jesus as the fulfillment and extension of Israel's prophetic tradition. This is anticipated in Mary's response to the angel Gabriel at the time of the annunciation: "[God] has shown strength with his arm; he has scattered the proud in the thoughts of their hearts. He has brought down the powerful from their thrones, and lifted up the lowly; he has filled the hungry with good things, and sent the rich away empty" (Lk 1:51-53). Note that Mary's images are those of social upheaval, not of a privatized gospel directed only toward inner peace and personal salvation.

Some 30 years later, according to Luke, Jesus connected his ministry to that of the Old Testament prophets by reading from the book of Isaiah: "[Jesus] stood up to read, and the scroll of the prophet Isaiah was given to him. He unrolled the scroll and found the place where it was written: 'The Spirit of the Lord is upon me, because he has anointed me to bring good news to the poor. He has sent me to proclaim release to the captives and recovery of sight to the blind, to let the oppressed go free, to proclaim the year of the Lord's favor'" (Lk 4:16-19, quoting Isa 61:1-2).

Later that day in Nazareth, Jesus referred to himself as a prophet. At Caesarea Philippi, when Jesus asked his disciples what people were saying about him, they replied that many people were calling him a prophet (Mt 16:14; Mk 8:28; Lk 9:19). On another occasion, addressing the increasing political resistance to his ministry in Galilee, Jesus said, "I must be on my way, because it is impossible for a prophet to be killed outside of Jerusalem. Jerusalem, Jerusalem, the city that kills the prophets and stones those who are sent to it" (Lk 13:33-34). When Jesus entered Jerusalem on Palm Sunday, the crowds shouted, "This is the prophet Jesus from Nazareth" (Mt 21:11). (Other passages underscoring the popular perception of Jesus as a prophet include Mark 6:15; Luke 7:16, 39; 24:19; and John 4:19; 9:17.)

The Gospels include many accounts of Jesus speaking to and healing people whom the religious authorities considered outcasts and outsiders - for example, women, people with leprosy and possessed by "demons," and Samaritans. His teaching and parables repeatedly challenged the religious leaders about interpretation of God's law. Luke 14:1-5 recounts Jesus' healing a man on the Sabbath and challenging the Pharisees and lawyers who questioned his actions. All of the Gospels tell of Jesus' dramatic "cleansing" of the temple in Jerusalem. He turned over the moneychangers' tables and took a whip to drive out the animals that were there to be sold for temple sacrifices. "Stop making my father's house a marketplace!" he demanded (Jn 2:13-17).

The prophetic tradition was foundational to Jesus' self-understanding and the response of others to his ministry - a ministry that was embraced by those who were marginalized but rejected by those in power.

Personal Reflection

1. What people, known to you personally or through the news, come to your mind as contemporary prophets?

2. How are contemporary prophets resisted and discredited?

3. Write a brief Help Wanted ad for a prophet. You will have a chance to share this if you choose when the group meets.

4. What is your response to the assertion that Jesus' ministry is a continuation of prophetic tradition?

5. Review some of Jesus' parables and teachings in Luke 12-21, noting the power structures and lifestyles he challenged and the positive changes he attempted to foster.

Distinguishing between Charity and Justice

The public church (Quadrant D) engages two significant kinds of social activity. The first is *social outreach,* represented by acts of mercy and charity in response to immediate needs of people for food, clothing, shelter, transportation, education, medical care, and so forth. It is important to drive someone to a doctor's appointment, to help at the food shelf, to collect books and care packages for a homeless shelter, or to tutor a child who is lagging behind at school. We know such activities are included in Jesus' declaration that serving the needs of the least of these is the same as doing something directly for Jesus (Mt 25). The need is clearly defined, and we see instant, tangible results. These results, however, do not solve possible underlying problems, and therefore the needs continue.

Social justice ministry, the second part of Quadrant D, addresses the root causes of hunger, poverty, and powerlessness that often lie in institutions and social systems. Social justice ministry tackles complex issues, such as establishing a living wage or addressing inequitable education opportunities, in an effort to effect change and long-term solutions. It involves analyzing the issues, strategizing responses, advocacy, and other actions. This is hard work. It is often controversial. Problems may be difficult to define; answers are elusive and varied. The results of social change may be ambiguous or not apparent for a long time. Vested interests threatened by social justice activities are apt to conceal or confuse the findings of researchers, malign those asking the questions, and resist reforms. The late Brazilian Archbishop Dom Helder Camara described such resistance this way: "When I feed the poor they call me a saint, but when I ask why they are poor, they call me a communist."

Both social outreach and social justice ministry are essential to the calling and mission of Christ's church. If the church limits its public activity to charitable relief alone, it may prolong underlying unjust conditions and avoid the prophetic confrontation necessary to evoke change in social structures. A church that limits its public activity to advocacy alone will not have the opportunity to interact with and really come to know the needs and aspirations of the people whose interests they claim to represent. A church operating on all cylinders will be fully engaged in both kinds of Quadrant D endeavors and also the other quadrants.

Personal Reflection

1. How are you involved in social outreach, that is, acts of charity and mercy? How is your church involved?

2. How are you involved in social justice ministry - studying social issues and taking action such as advocacy? How is your church involved?

3. Complete the following sentence: Social justice ministry in my church...

4. Then think of a situation, issue, or abuse that, in the light of biblical teaching and the life and ministry of Jesus, you think is displeasing to God. Complete the sentences on the following page as if you were a modern-day prophet speaking for God.

Thus says the Lord to *(for example, a contemporary leader, group, industry, or local, state, or national governing body)*

I see *(what's wrong)*

This is causing *(the result or impact of this wrong)*

I will *(what the consequences will be if this continues)*

You must *(what actions are necessary to correct this wrong)*

If you do this *(the positive result of making the required changes)*

If you don't do this *(the negative results of not making changes)*

You will be invited to share your prophetic announcement at the next group meeting.

Called to Follow Jesus

The church's social justice ministry continues a tradition of faithfulness to its biblical roots and the calling to follow Jesus Christ into the world. Because nearly all churches and many of their members readily engage in charitable endeavors, this study focuses on the more threatening, complicated, and often neglected social justice part of the church's public ministry.

Session Three
Perspective Makes a Difference

An ancient fable tells of six blind men who describe their first experience with an elephant. "The elephant is like a wall," says the one who held his hands up to the animal's side. "The elephant is like a spear," suggests the one who grabbed its tusk. "The elephant is like a snake," says the one holding its trunk. "No, the elephant is like a tree," reports the one with his arms around its leg. "The elephant is a fanlike creature," asserts the one holding the elephant's ear. "No, the elephant is like a rope," says the one who holds the elephant's tail. (Countless versions of this ancient fable can be found in Hindu, Islamic, Buddhist, and other traditions. The images used here are based on John Godfrey Saxe's poem "Blind Men and the Elephant.")

Because we are outside the story and have access to the big picture, we can easily see how ridiculous it is for the six men to claim that their limited, partial experience represents the whole elephant. It's harder to see this same dynamic at work when our own experiences and assumptions are involved. While we may find the story about the blind men and the elephant humorous, we are mystified and aggravated when others don't see our certainties in the same way we do.

In this session you will identify some of your own blind spots, limited knowledge, and perceptions using the concepts of social location and designed blindness. With other participants in your study group, you will begin to look at the impact of these realities on individuals and communities.

Social Location

Sociologists refer to the different vantage points occupied by the blind men - and indeed all of us - as issues related to social location. Social location refers to the cluster of factors and circumstances such as age, education, and race that define and limit our experiences. Typical factors associated with social location include the following descriptors:

Race

Economic class

Gender

Education level

Age

Physical abilities and disabilities

Nationality

Sexual orientation

Religion

Geographical setting

Social location affects the assumptions we make about life and the way we interpret what goes on around us. Social location often determines the opportunities we do or do not have in life as well as the resources and support available to us. The child of a Mexican immigrant growing up in Los Angeles will experience "American opportunity" very differently from the child of college graduates growing up in the Virginia suburbs of Washington, D.C. The black businessman who is arrested as a suspect in a nearby bank robbery while he is innocently putting oil in his Jaguar at a gas station in a white neighborhood will describe "police security" differently than local residents would. Our social location deeply affects what we experience in life and what we think, feel, and expect in response to those experiences. The tension between "Black lives matter" and "All lives matter" reflects in part perspectives stemming from different social locations.

Whether people are aware of it or not, their social location inevitably affects their perceptions and interpretations. Recognizing our social location gives each of us clues for acquiring greater self-awareness and understanding of others and how their experience may be different than our own. Through examining our social location, we can achieve a better picture of the whole "elephant."

Ignoring social location is dangerous. Whenever a society makes generalizations based on the unexamined assumptions of one group's social location and imposes its conclusions on others through its expectations, laws, and policies, injustice is the frequent result. Since in a democracy politics and government ideally focus on planning together for the common good, and because following Jesus compels Christians to love their neighbors as themselves, we need to understand the reality and implications of social location. Current explications of *white privilege*, which are challenging many of us to deepen our awareness about this aspect of racism, is a good example of social location related consciousness raising.

Personal Reflection

Make some notes next to the social location factors listed above to define your own social location. Think about the implications of that location and then complete sentences to reflect various implications related to your social location. For example: Because I am white, I go unnoticed in white upper-class neighborhoods. Because I am of Palestinian descent, I often get stopped in airports. Because I am in a wheelchair, people talk to me slowly in a raised voice.

Because I...

I....

Because I...

I...

Because I...

I...

At your next group session, you will have the opportunity to share some of these sentences as you choose.

Designed Blindness

Self-confidence is important for personal effectiveness and the development of healthy relationships, but when self-confidence inflates itself into total certainty, a person's growth becomes stunted by an inability to take in new information and reexamine assumptions. Learning depends upon exposure to ideas that expand a person's horizons, but the human tendency is to protect ourselves from anything that threatens our comfort level or requires us to change. Sadly, this seems particularly true in matters of religion and politics that have far-reaching effects on social structures.

Former United Nations Secretary-General Kofi Annan, in his Nobel Peace Prize acceptance speech, described such certainty this way: "The idea that there is one people in possession of the truth, one answer to the world's ills or one solution to humanity's needs has done untold harm throughout history" {*Newsweek,* December 17, 2001). And on the other end of the scale is the *Peanuts* cartoon where Charlie Brown approaches Snoopy who is typing away on top of his doghouse. Charlie says, "I hear you're writing a book on Theology. I hope you have a good title." *I have a perfect title,* Snoopy thinks to himself: *Has It Ever Occurred to You that You Might Be Wrong?* That is a healthy question for all of us to keep in mind, even as we speak out and make commitments for what we believe and value.

A term for the human tendency toward static, closed thinking is "designed blindness." In her book *Learning While Leading,* Anita Farber-Robertson defines designed blindness as the "choice, conscious or otherwise, to be unaware of that which is available to be known to us" (p. 3). In other words, "I've made up my mind, don't bother me with facts." Even with minimal knowledge of psychology, we can recognize the tricks we use to maintain this posture, including the following common defense mechanisms:

Rationalizing: We justify our own acts and opinions by ascribing them to causes that seem valid but are not verified. For example, he says, "I didn't go visit Paul while he was in prison because he would be embarrassed to have me see him in that setting." Actually, Paul wanted visitors, but the speaker didn't want to take the time and trouble to arrange the visit.

Minimizing: She says, "No, I didn't go. It was no big deal." In fact, the occasion was very important to her and she was disappointed and hurt not to be invited.

Avoidance: "I'm not interested in that." We can hang onto any stereotype we choose if we never encounter or learn more about the person, group, or situation embraced by our false preconceptions.

Denial: "I never said that!" In fact, he did actually say that.

Blaming: "They should not have been there in the first place." The speaker, who started a fight, is defending himself by casting responsibility for it on others.

Attacking: "You have no right to say that. You can't begin to prove it. You don't even have a college education." The speaker, whose job performance is below average, is putting down the person giving the appraisal instead of taking in the feedback.

Projection: "He is so self-centered." A narcissistic speaker finds her own faults and shortcomings in others.

Distorted comparison: "I believe in equal opportunity for everyone. You are preventing immigrants from assimilating by pushing ESL programs." The speaker, a native born US citizen, is mixing apples and oranges to oppose a budget expenditure.

   One of my favorite Sunday morning comments came after a sermon about psychological projection based on the story in 2 Samuel about David's vehement condemnation of the rich man who took the poor man's only ewe instead of using one from his own large flock (12:1-9). After worship the departing parishioner said, "That was a good sermon. I wish my sister could hear it." She paused for a second, and then, recognizing that she was voicing a perfect example of projection, we both laughed. As Jesus noted, we tend to worry a lot about the splinters in others' eyes when we should focus on the log in our own eye; then we can see better how to help someone else (Mt 7:4-5; Lk 6:41-42).

Personal Reflection

1. Recall a time when you misjudged a person or situation. How did you respond?

2. What blind spots have you discovered about yourself?

Faith Practices Expanding our Horizons

Several current authors - philosopher Sam Harris *(Letter to a Christian Nation),* biologist Richard Dawkins *(The God Delusion),* and journalist Christopher Hitchens *(God Is Not Great: How Religion Poisons Everything),* among others - have recently joined the long historical list of critics who assert that Christianity is a closed-minded religion. Regretfully, from the Inquisition to the Salem, Massachusetts, witch-hunts to the present day, there is ample data for them to draw upon. Proclaimed faith convictions do sometimes serve as a respectable veneer for ignorance, fear, and prejudice. Such behavior, however, misrepresents the gospel of Jesus Christ and distorts some of the most enduring teachings of the church. Let us briefly consider four basic practices of Christian faith that speak to these matters: humility, repentance, accepting God's grace, and hospitality.

1. Humility

The word *humility* is often associated with feeling bad about oneself while deferring to others or making oneself a doormat for people to walk over. But true humility has to do with being open to learning and having the willingness to accept feedback from others. It is about knowing our own limitations and accepting our need for help. The basis for this humility is recognizing our rightful place in the scheme of God's world. That is the lesson embodied in this story from Thomas Merton's *Wisdom of the Desert:*

Some elders once came to Abbot Anthony, and there was with them also Abbot Joseph. Wishing to test them, Abbot Anthony brought the conversation around to the Holy Scriptures. And he began from the youngest to ask them the meaning of this or that text. Each one replied as best he could, but Abbot Anthony said to them: You have not got it yet. After them all he asked Abbot Joseph: What about you? What do you say this text means? Abbot Joseph replied: I know not! Then Abbot Anthony said: Truly Abbot Joseph alone has found the way, for he replies that he knows not (quoted by Kathleen Norris in Amazing Grace, p. 333).

Humility is a path to mental health as well as to wisdom. "We see," as the apostle Paul wrote to Jesus' followers in Corinth, only "in a mirror, dimly (1 Cor 13:12). "For God's foolishness is wiser than human wisdom, and God's weakness is stronger than human strength" (1 Cor 1:25).

2. Repentance

Another central practice of Christians through the ages is repentance, which means to turn around, to change direction, or to adjust one's attitude. New experiences and insights can provide the stimulus for repentance. In a powerful scene from *Amazing Grace,* a movie about the abolition of slavery in the British Empire, reformer William Wilberforce organizes an afternoon boating party on the Thames River for some prominent members of Parliament and their wives. Wilberforce shrewdly charts a course that takes them by the stench and chains of a recently arrived slave ship. Their visceral reaction to this silent testimony to the inhumane realities of slave trading changed many minds. Similarly, Harriet Beecher Stowe's *Uncle Tom's Cabin* brought many of its readers into the American abolitionist movement. Hearing the personal stories of refugees, watching an execution, working with a gay person, or losing a job may very likely alter or even "turn around" one's opinions about immigration, capital punishment, gay rights, and welfare benefits.

3. Accepting God's Grace

Christians understand grace as the unmerited love and forgiveness of God. The assurance of God's grace frees us to face the truth about ourselves. Many familiar prayers of confession, such as those quoted below, begin by affirming trust in God's grace:

"Gracious God, you have promised to receive us when we come to you . .." *(Book of Worship,* p. 530).

"Almighty God, Spirit of purity and grace, whose salvation is never far from the contrite heart..." *(Book of Worship,* p. 531).

"If we confess our sins, God is faithful and just, and will forgive our sins and cleanse us from every kind of wrong" *(Book of Common Prayer).*

It is hard to admit our mistakes, to see ourselves in a bad light, to acknowledge that we have invested ourselves in beliefs, causes, and pursuits that contradict God's love and violate God's justice. The promise of God's grace, the vision of the waiting father's outstretched arms ready to receive the wayward child who had squandered his resources, the assurance that *nothing* on earth or beyond will ever separate us from God's love - these and countless other biblical images stand as ever-present invitations to open ourselves to the search for a broader and deeper truth. That search can both strengthen our faith and embolden us to engage in the public activity of social justice ministry.

4. Hospitality

We receive "the other" in response to God's gracious openness to us. Israel's ancient laws repeatedly admonished people to provide for sojourners in their land because they too had been aliens in the land of Egypt (Deut 23:7). Jesus condemned our failure to extend to others the grace we have received by telling a parable about the unmerciful servant who failed to forgive the small debt of a fellow servant even after his master had forgiven him a very large debt (Mt 18:23-35).

"The other" includes those we consider strangers. The author of Hebrews, referring to the visitors entertained by Abraham from the Genesis 18 account, writes: "Let mutual love continue. Do not neglect to show hospitality to strangers, for by doing that some have entertained angels without knowing it" (Heb 13:1-2). In a world where differences so often lead to fear and violence rather than to increased mutual understanding, it seems quite appropriate to identify those who expand our experience base as angels to be entertained.

Elizabeth Canham, an Episcopal priest and retreat leader, summarizes the spirit of hospitality that pervades the Rule of Benedict, written for sixth-century monastics, in her *Weavings* article "A School for the Lord's Service." She writes, "People do not enter our lives to be coerced or manipulated, but to enrich us by their differences, and to be graciously received in the name of Christ" (January-February 1994, p. 13).

Seeing Sisters and Brothers

A vision of peace based on mutually caring human relationships fostered by humility, repentance, grace, and hospitality is a common element in all of the world's major faith traditions. This story comes from Martin Buber's collection, *Tales of the Hasidim:*

> *An ancient rabbi once asked his pupils how they could tell when the night had ended and day had begun. "Could it be," asked one student, "when you can see an animal in the distance and can tell whether it is a sheep or a dog?" "No," answered the rabbi. Another asked, "Is it when you can look at a tree in the distance and tell whether it's a fig or a peach tree?" "No," answered the rabbi. "Then when is it?" the pupils demanded. "It is when you can look on the face of any woman or man and see your sister or brother. Because if you cannot see this, then it does not matter what time it is, it is still night."*

The affirmation that we are all children of the same God and members of one human family forever compels us to listen to one another in order to know our own story more fully.

Personal Reflection

1. When have you had an "aha" experience that changed your thinking about an issue? What caused it? How did it change you? In what ways did the experience draw out humility, repentance, accepting God's grace, or hospitality?

2. Immigration is a contentious issue in the United States today. How might the Christian practices identified in this section inform thoughts and feelings about this issue?

3. Write a short prayer expressing your own response to these thoughts about humility, repentance, accepting God's grace, and hospitality.

Opening Ourselves to the Gifts of Others

We hear a lot today about the information explosion and how interconnected the world has become. Far too many of us, however, retrieve that information selectively as we restrict our reading, watching, and listening to those who share our viewpoints and biases. Harvard professor Diana Eck, author of *A New Religious America: How a "Christian Country" Has Become the World's Most Religiously Diverse Nation,* suggests that, while diversity is now this country's reality, real pluralism - that is, the interaction of diverse people with one another - is less evident. In an interview with *Religion and Ethics Newsweekly* she explained:

> *Pluralism really means what we do with all the diversity that is ours, how we engage with it, if we engage with it. It means not just the ghettoization of diversity ... it means addressing diversity, trying to build the bridges of communication and traffic that enable our diversity to build relationships ... we really need to understand more of who we are when we say, "We the people of the United States." That's a pretty big statement, and we need to be able to have some sense of who these neighbors are (April 26, 2002).*

Eck reminds us that it takes intentional effort for us to learn the truth from other perspectives, the kind of truth that can set us free from the barriers of social location and our limited contexts.

In his book *God's Tapestry: Understanding and Celebrating Differences,* professor and multicultural consultant William M. Kondrath suggests guidelines for recognizing and valuing differences. The first one is to "try on." He describes the process of shopping for a new pair of shoes as an analogy for exploring new ideas. We go into a store, he says, or more than one store, and try on several pairs of shoes, walking around a bit to get the feel of them, looking in the mirror, and comparing back and forth. We may leave with a pair of new shoes or we may leave with only the same shoes we had when we walked in. His point is that "to try on an idea does not mean that I have to accept the idea I am being asked to examine. It does mean that I am willing to consider or reconsider something from a viewpoint that I have not considered before, or perhaps have previously considered and rejected" (pp. 5-6).

The Greek philosopher Epictetus (AD 55-ca. 135) is remembered for saying, "We have two ears and one mouth so that we can listen twice as much as we speak." Writing at about the same time, the author of the letter of James exhorts, "You must understand this, my beloved: let everyone be quick to listen, slow to speak" (1:19). Good listening is a sign of caring and respect. It is essential for meaningful relationships to develop and for learning to take place.

We do not feel cared about when someone keeps interrupting us while we are talking. And we are not really listening to someone else if we're already composing our response or evaluating what the speaker is saying through the lens of our own experience. Even giving good advice can inhibit the speaker's own process. Using a metaphor from Befriender Ministry, a listening ministry for lay pastoral care, we need to "empty our own cup" in order to be fully present to another while listening to their story. This means letting go of any agenda we may have for this person.

Communications books and trainers may use different terminology, but they all emphasize the importance of these basic listening skills:

- Focus on the speaker, using eye contact and other attentive body language such as nodding one's head and putting all other work aside. (Note: It takes extra time and effort to stay focused when the speaker has an unfamiliar accent or limited English skills.)

- Express your interest. Encourage the speaker to continue.

- Ask open-ended questions that elicit fuller disclosure of the speaker's experience and perceptions.

- Listen respectfully.

- Try to understand the speaker's point of view even when you don't agree with that point of view or have a very different experience.

This kind of listening reduces tension and fosters honest relationships where differences can be productively and mutually explored.

Personal Reflection

1. Think of a time when you really made an effort to listen to someone else. What did you learn from that experience?

2. At their best, novels, movies, and plays transport us into other worlds. They enable us to walk in someone else's shoes and hear that person's story. Think of a movie, book, or play that did this for you. What did you learn? How has that learning affected your thinking? How has it affected your behavior?

3. Your group will hear from a guest speaker from a social location different from the majority of people in your group. Based on what you know about yourself and what your study leader tells you about the guest, what listening skill do you especially want to practice during the next session? Prepare an open-ended question to ask the guest speaker.

4. If you could remember only one idea prompted by reading Session 3, what would it be?

Seeing and Listening

Up to this point in the study, the focus has been on building a foundation for your church's involvement in social ministry. This session looked at the finitude of human perceptions, particularly your own, and the importance of being open to the experiences and viewpoints of others. The next session will look at how to prepare yourself and your congregation to be effective advocates for social justice.

Session Four

Sowing Seeds for Justice

Jesus told several parables comparing God's work in the world to the planting of seeds. The kingdom of God, Jesus might say, embraces many fields and many crops. Numerous factors are involved, including hostile forces of resistance, such as rocks, bad soil, and birds that snatch the seed, as well as the benevolent, growth-producing forces of air, rain, and sunshine. While specific outcomes at the level of individual seeds are unpredictable, Jesus assured his disciples then and now that a bountiful harvest would be realized (a loose paraphrase of Matthew 13). The faithfulness of the sower in all seasons and circumstances is crucial.

Long before Jesus' time, the prophet Isaiah had used a sowing metaphor to describe the failed calling of Israel to be in a special covenant with God that would produce a vineyard where justice and righteousness flourished. In the form of a love song to God's chosen people, Isaiah wrote:

> *My beloved had a vineyard on a very fertile hill.*
> *He dug it and cleared it of stones, and planted it with choice vines;...*
> *He expected it to yield grapes, but it yielded wild grapes....*
> *For the vineyard of the Lord of hosts is the house of Israel,*
> *and the people of Judah are his pleasant planting;*
> *he expected justice, but saw bloodshed;*
> *righteousness, but heard a cry!* (Isa 5:1, 2, 7)

This session explores how the seeds of personal sensitivity to matters of justice are sown through individual experiences and how the church can provide and interpret such experiences through its evangelical heritage and prophetic calling in the world. In today's world, social justice ministry is a formidable calling and takes time.

Born Activists and Converted Advocates

Community organizer Rev. Alexia Salvatierra, executive director of
Clergy and Laity United for Economic Justice Los Angeles (CLUE LA),
asserts that one out of ten adults is a "born activist," which she defines as
someone who instinctively feels the pain of others as his or her own and
devotes themselves to alleviating the source(s) of that pain. Salvatierra
goes on to point out that these born activists don't know what it's like *not*
to be a born activist. When we consider that the remaining 90 percent need
to learn much of what is innately obvious to "born activists," we can begin
to understand the disconnect we often find between these two groups in
our congregations.

Both of these groups can be found in many congregations. However, they
often coexist without meaningful interaction that might facilitate mutual
understanding, growth, and effectiveness. The 10 percent born activists are
more apt to recognize injustice and to hear the voices of those affected by it.
They readily engage in controversial issues when they perceive a need for
change. They may become impatient, judgmental, and dismissive of those
who just don't "get it." The other 90 percent tend to be more accepting of the
status quo because they see it as normative. They are often uncomfortable
with the born activists, whom they may see as disruptive and fanatical. It will
take these "non-born activists" longer to buy into justice-based arguments.
When they do engage, their involvement is likely to take different forms.

In reality, two such clearly defined groups do not exist; rather, the people
in most churches are spread across a continuum of perceptions and attitudes.
Nonetheless, people in most churches can readily name "the activists." The
non-born activists are typically found in the mainstream of the church's
leadership and program planning while the born activists are on the margins.
The non-born activists on the inside tolerate the presence of the born activists
as long as they don't make waves. Consequently, much of the born activists'
outreach and advocacy is pursued outside the church in the individual's daily
life (Quadrant C).

The term *born activist* is somewhat misleading because the ability to empathize and the will to act on behalf of powerless people and unpopular causes is not part of our DNA. This awareness and these impulses grow out of personal experience. It's a matter of nurture, not nature. I prefer the word *advocate* to *activist* because *activist* has a militant connotation that can turn others off and encourage unnecessary resistance. Through its Latin root *vocare*, the word *advocate* highlights the sense of being called to argue or plead for the cause or interests of another, which seems closer to the public role of the church on behalf of social justice. This is not in anyway to discount the importance of *activists* because action is always the bottom line.

We must continually remind ourselves that all four quadrants are essential for faithful witness to the gospel of Jesus Christ. The quadrants do not compete with each other - they mutually support each other. Just as the same cardiovascular system sustains every part of the body, so the same Spirit enlivens the life and ministry of every quadrant. As the apostle Paul wisely observed: "Now there are varieties of gifts, but the same Spirit; and there are varieties of services, but the same Lord; and there are varieties of activities, but it is the same God who activates all of them in everyone" (1 Cor 12:4-6).

This study emphasizes the social justice part of Quadrant D because that is what tends to be neglected in most churches. The born activists in our churches and the "to-be-converted" advocates need to find and learn to trust each other for their mutual learning and support.

Personal Reflection

1. To what extent do you see yourself as a born activist and why do you think this is or is not so?

2. What tensions around social justice ministry have you experienced in your church?

Nurturing Awareness: How to Prepare the Soil

The role that experience plays in fostering awareness of social injustice and inspiring a personal response to it is evident in sociologist Dieter Hessel's list of "Key Factors Motivating Social Justice Awareness" in *Social Ministry* (p. 44):

Early exposure to social justice teaching. I think of my friend Sandy who attended a Catholic school that was permeated with social justice teachings and the activism of Dorothy Day.

Encounter with other cultures. Missionaries and their children, as well as people in other professions that offer long-term exposure to other cultures on a daily basis, often acquire a broader frame of reference about what is "normal."

Personal experience or exposure to oppression. Experiencing the effects of racism, sexism, poverty, homophobia, and other forms of oppression, personally or through the circumstances of someone you know and love, strikes a deeper chord than simply reading about it. The parent of a gay child becomes an advocate for gay rights. A horrific racist remark I overheard when I was seven or eight years old made a lifelong impression on me.

Example of admired leaders. Whether it's a world-renowned figure such as Mahatma Gandhi, Elizabeth Cady Stanton, Martin Luther King Jr., or Dietrich Bonhoeffer, or the woman in a local church who persistently asked the hard questions that others wanted to skip over, it helps to have models we can relate to.

Fresh theological insights. Through a sermon, a conversation, a book, or an interior "aha" moment, we are sometimes awakened to new awareness of God's intentions for us and for the world. It often takes just the right explanation at the right time in a person's life to break through his or her indifference, confusion, or designed blindness.

Participation in new forms of action. I think of my friend Grant from Illinois who took his teenage son to march in Selma, Alabama, and they both became lifelong advocates for equal rights. Indifferent neighbors have become converted advocates after attending a rally at the invitation of a friend.

Being part of a supportive community. This epitomizes the difference between working for social justice as an individual (Quadrant C) and as part of a church community (Quadrant D). The sharing of ideas and experiences; the friends we make working together; and shared growth in awareness, mutual encouragement, and affirmation keep us motivated to stay involved.

Experiencing success and perceiving effectiveness. Grassroots communities who tackle ingrained social structures and powerful institutions are more likely to succeed when they take manageable steps and build on small gains. The widely publicized boycotts of Nestle in the 1970s and, more recently, Taco Bell, come to mind. The Montgomery, Alabama bus boycott galvanized the civil rights movement in the United States.

The above factors typically overlap to foster concern and meaningful action for social justice. The church can positively affect the presence of these factors in the lives of its members. Indeed, one way is by making the Christian formation of moral consciousness a major function of the church - one that is ongoing, comprehensive, and owned by every corner and level of the congregation.

During World War II, hundreds of Jews were protected and aided in getting to safety in Switzerland by the people of Le Chambon, a small village in southern France. Years later Holocaust researcher Philip Hallie sought to understand the unique response of this community despite the great danger to themselves, describing his findings in his book *Lest Innocent Blood Be Shed: The Story of the Village of Le Chambon and How Goodness Happened There.* He learned that this was a Huguenot community whose own long history was replete with religious persecution. When he asked surviving residents of Le Chambon how such moral sensitivity to the plight of the Jews and the courage to help them could be instilled in other people and places, the response he most often received was, "It takes generations to prepare" (as told by Bruce C. Birch and Larry L. Rasmussen, *Bible and Ethics in the Christian Life,* Augsburg Fortress, 1989, p. 124).

The church is called to prepare people - generation after generation - to take notice of the powerless and to respond to their needs in Christian love. Through its worship, scriptures, preaching, teaching, liturgy, outreach, pastoral care, programs, fellowship, witness, and every other aspect of its life, the church seeks to bring the living word of God into the present. And as the community gathers to share these things, a tradition is extended and an identity is formed. God's people are preparing the soil for sowing seeds for justice.

Personal Reflection

Make notes below as to how strongly Dieter Hessel's key factors have been present in your own life; what stories or memories, if any, are triggered by thinking about these factors; and where you see these factors present in the current life of your congregation as a whole.

Early exposure to social justice teaching

How present in your early life (use 1-5 check marks):

Associated memory or story:

Where present in your congregation:

Encounter with other cultures

How present in your early life (use 1-5 check marks):

Associated memory or story:

Where present in your congregation:

Personal experience or exposure to oppression

How present in your early life (use 1-5 check marks):

Associated memory or story:

Where present in your congregation:

Example of admired leaders

How present in your early life (use 1-5 check marks):

Associated memory or story:

Where present in your congregation:

Fresh theological insights

How present in your early life (use 1-5 check marks):

Associated memory or story:

Where present in your congregation:

Participation in new forms of action

How present in your early life (use 1-5 check marks):

Associated memory or story:

Where present in your congregation:

Being part of a supportive community

How present in your early life (use 1-5 check marks):

Associated memory or story:

Where present in your congregation:

Experiencing success and perceiving effectiveness

How present in your early life (use 1-5 check marks):

Associated memory or story:

Where present in your congregation:

At the next group session you will have the opportunity to discuss some of these observations as you choose.

Who Is My Neighbor?

After Cain murdered his brother Abel, God asked, "Where is your brother Abel?" Cain attempted to side-step God's searching inquiry with the cavalier response, "Am I my brother's keeper?" (Gen 4:9). This is a rhetorical question for biblical faith to which the answer has always been an unequivocal "Yes!" When the lawyer asked Jesus to define who was the neighbor we are commanded to love, Jesus expanded the concept of neighbor by telling the parable of the good Samaritan (Lk 10:29-37). Concern for the widows, orphans, and aliens in the land is reflected throughout the Hebrew and Christian scriptures. It reverberates in prophetic judgments denouncing the haves for their neglect of the have-nots. It underlies the one out of every sixteen verses of the New Testament that address the plight of the poor.

Biblical faith compels the church's commitment to social ministry. Yet the world today is two thousand years removed from the biblical world, which means that the application of biblical mandates needs to be reaffirmed for these times and circumstances, just as Jesus did in his time. Six aspects of contemporary life increase the urgency and scope of the public role of the church: (1) complex issues, (2) individualism, (3) psychological distance, (4) globalization, (5) environmental stewardship, and (6) limited resources. In today's world we need to be sowing seeds in a larger and larger garden because our neighbors live all around the world!

1. Complex Issues

The really big issues that affect people's everyday lives - poverty, education, great disparity of assets and opportunity, health care, housing, unemployment, hunger, climate change, and violence - are deeply entrenched and may seem overwhelming in their complexity. Most of us want to be certain about something before we stick our necks out, so it's easy for us "amateurs" to defer to the "experts." Everyone - politicians, corporations, governments, and church people - tends to paint his or her actions and ambitions in the best possible light, making it hard for us to know what to believe and whom to trust.

In the face of daunting, widespread problems and competing interests, taking action or imagining how one small group can have much impact can be difficult. But we in the church have a unique perspective, and there are many churches in many places around the world. The answer is to act with thoughtful focus, purpose, and faithfulness, trusting that God will use our best efforts. And as we act, we learn more and can correct mistakes and fine-tune our objectives. Jesus' parable of the talents (Mt 25:14-30; Lk 19:12-27) suggests that God is best served when we act boldly with what we have, rather than allow ourselves to be paralyzed by fear.

2. Individualism

In the Bible the word *you* is usually plural because it addresses the community, the people of God. The modern world, however, tends to hear *you* as an individual. In American culture, we hear far more about individual rights and personal growth than we do about the common good. Children are encouraged to develop self-esteem. Parents are more worried about getting their own child into the best schools than they are about improving the state of education for everyone's children. Voices of a faith that embraces the vision of "the one family of God" are needed to counter the fierce individualism of our society. I once heard a preacher say that we need to think like Southerners in order to hear the Bible correctly: When it says *you*, it really means *y'all.*

3. Psychological Distance

Our attention is instinctively attracted to the people and issues that are closest to us or easiest for us to identify with. In 1999 the story of Elian Gonzalez, a five-year-old Cuban boy who was rescued while drifting for two days in an inner tube on the Atlantic Ocean, captured the world's attention. He and thirteen other immigrants had left Cuba in a small boat. They were headed to Florida when their boat sank and most of the other passengers drowned, including Elian's mother. For months people across the United States followed the ensuing, highly politicized custody case between his father in Cuba and more distant expatriate family members in Miami's Little Havana, until the child returned to Cuba with his father. During the same time, hundreds of thousands of politically motivated, unprosecuted deaths, disappearances, and incidents of torture occurring in Central America went unnoticed by the vast majority of Americans.

When someone we identify with is affected by an injustice, we are motivated to respond, but large groups of people who suffer from systemic injustices tend to remain nameless and escape our concern. Long-term issues that desperately need to be addressed such as climate change, energy conservation, and sustainable sources tend to become problems for somebody else or some other time. In the words of Dan Ariely, a professor of behavioral economics at Duke University, "We should really care about the long-term well-being of the planet but when we get up in the morning it's very hard to motivate ourselves."

A few stories may come to us and touch us personally. Most of the time, however, if we are to see and hear these people, we need to alter our pathways and seek out these stories, then take the time to listen attentively. We need to move outside our social location. The principle of solidarity, based on the interconnectedness of all humanity, teaches us to act intentionally where we are, both to change our immediate environment and to serve as a sign of standing with those who seem so far away. Frederick Buechner said, "The life I touch for good or ill will touch another life, and that in turn another, until who knows where the trembling stops or in what far place my touch will be felt."

As Session 3 stressed, there are many things you and your church can do to learn more about the plight of those who are now nameless to you but never to God, thereby expanding your awareness and bringing others, of whom you have been unaware, into psychologically closer distances.

4. Globalization

"It's a Small World" was a popular song in the early seventies. More recently, journalist Thomas L. Friedman uses a different metaphor in his book *The World Is Flat*. The earth is flat in the sense that it has become a level playing field. Advances in technology and communication have removed barriers to international competition, allowing countries around the world to win a share of global markets. The economic, social, cultural, environmental, and political impacts of globalization are complex and vigorously disputed. Have free trade treaties reduced world poverty or increased it? How has globalization affected labor and working conditions? What about environmental considerations? How have near-instant global communications and technological innovations affected world development?

A 2015 global wealth report (from inequality.org) notes that 71% of the world holds only 3% of global wealth. At the other end of the scale, 8.1% of the global population owns 84.6% of global wealth and a miniscule .004% of the world population holds 12.8% of total global wealth. In January 2017, the global anti-poverty movement Oxfam reported that the world's eight richest men own as much wealth as the 3.6 billion people comprising the poorest half of the world's population combined.

Globalization broadens and complicates the arena that a public church must address. However, as Professor William T. Cavanaugh notes in his book *Theopolitical Imagination,* globalization also offers new opportunities for reimagining the planet, moving from an image of nationally divided interests to one of a single Eucharistic vision of one world table. Globalization is inevitable. The challenge is how to minimize its negative impacts and maximize its possibilities for good. This is Quadrant D work for the church!

5. Environmental Stewardship
The first Earth Day in the United States was celebrated in 1970. Until that time most Americans had taken clean water, air, and soil for granted, although the Soil Conservation Service had been a permanent agency within the Department of Agriculture since 1935. Today global warming is a major and growing concern as scientists move to consensus that the problem is real and that human activity is contributing to it.

Theologians of all stripes now reject the hierarchical understanding that the phrase "have dominion" in the Genesis creation story confers upon human beings the right to abuse creation. They pay more attention to the phrase "to till and to keep," emphasizing the profound interrelatedness of all creation. Christians are beginning to understand sustainability not only as a wise principle but also as a form of love for future generations.

Because economists predict that the most negative consequences of the environmental crisis will have their greatest impact on the world's poor, stewardship of creation is also an urgent issue of justice. Some still dispute these environmental tenets. Others talk the talk without making necessary changes in personal lifestyles and corporate policies. Our Christian heritage has much to say about sin, redemption, hope, and self-giving love. How will we embody these faith principles in all quadrants of our lives and in the public witness of Christ's church as part of our environmental stewardship?

6. Limited Resources

Social justice ministry takes time and energy out of crowded schedules and takes monetary resources out of budgets that are typically stretched. Too often social justice ministry is seen as an expendable extra rather than as an integral and essential part of being church. Immediate church family and institutional needs fill the radar screen and consume available resources.

Jesus, however, preached a gospel of abundance, not scarcity, to economically disadvantaged communities in an occupied country. To those who become preoccupied with personal affairs and institutional maintenance, Jesus might say, "What will it profit them to gain the whole world and forfeit their life?" (Mk 8:36). Surely churches in this prosperous nation who see social justice ministry as an integral part of who they are will find resources to follow the incarnate Christ into the world.

A Bigger Garden

These are big issues that can overwhelm us and tempt us to retreat into the safer stance of privatized religion. Perhaps this is what the discouraged prophet Isaiah was feeling when he lamented, "I have labored in vain, I have spent my strength for nothing and vanity" (Isa 49:4). But God replies by saying, "It is too light a thing that you should be my servant to raise up the tribes of Jacob and to restore the survivors of Israel; I will give you as a light to the nations, that my salvation may reach to the end of the earth" (Isa 49:6). When the people of God think small, God offers a fuller vision and a bigger challenge. Our faith, Jesus said, can move mountains of obstacles and impossibilities if we prepare the soil faithfully and sow seeds of hope and trust.

Personal Reflection

1. What feelings, questions, or concerns did the previous section "Who Is My Neighbor?" evoke for you?

2. In addition to the challenges already identified, what other contemporary challenges to social justice ministry come to mind?

Using Our Power

Many of us have ambiguous thoughts and feelings about power and the church. We were taught to sing about "baby Jesus meek and mild" and to see the adult Jesus being "led like a lamb to the slaughter" as a virtue to be imitated by individual Christians and the church. However, Rev. Hannah Brown, former associate pastor of Mayflower Church in Minneapolis, a church that has donated land and lobbied for workforce housing in the attractive, accessible, middle-class community surrounding the church, notes in a 2008 issue of the church's newsletter:

> The Bible is full of talk about power. A prophet proclaims, "As for me, I am filled with power, with the Spirit of the Lord, and with justice and might" (Micah 3:8). A psalmist reminds us, "The God of Israel gives strength and power to God's people" (Ps 68:35). Paul writes to the Christian community in Rome, saying: "I see no reason to be ashamed of the gospel; it is God's power, for in it is revealed the saving justice of God" (Rom 1:16-17).

> These words from our tradition can help us overcome our aversion to power. According to scripture, God has power. God grants this power to us and God's power is a tool for justice. Power without accountability or without a vision for the common good is dangerous. But power that is shared in our community, power built to create positive change, is not only good, but also essential to following God's call.

Pastor and civil rights activist William Sloane Coffin often quoted the famous maxim attributed to Lord Acton, "Power corrupts; and absolute power corrupts absolutely." But then Coffin goes on to say, "But failure to assume responsibility for power is also corrupting and devastating today in its effects. For evil is not so much the work of a few degenerate people or groups of people as it is the result of the indifference and negligence of the many" *(Credo,* p. 52).

Personal Reflection

How would you complete the following sentence?

My church has the power to...

Sowing the Seeds for Justice in Our Congregation

The congregation has a unique and important role in nurturing social justice awareness. The next session focuses on the relationship between church and state so that as your church undertakes social justice ministry in the political realm, it does so legally, appropriately, and effectively.

Session Five
God and Emperor: Discerning the Dividing Line

We might be tempted to think that the relationship between "church" and "state" was simpler in Jesus' time and place, --two thousand years ago in an occupied country, --but it was a dicey issue even then. When the Pharisees and Herodians asked Jesus if it was lawful for Jews to pay taxes to Caesar, Jesus asked whose image was on the coin. When they replied that it was the emperor's head, Jesus said, "Give therefore to the emperor the things that are the emperor's, and to God the things that are God's" (Mt 22:21; Mk 12:17).

Twenty centuries later the challenge of discerning in new times and settings what we owe to the state as citizens and what we owe to God as Christians raises difficult questions: How does our faith affect our participation in a democratic political process? What do we do when we perceive tensions between demands of "Caesar" and the calling of God? What happens when one group's understanding of God's will for the common good is at odds with that of another religious group?

Most people readily affirm that the separation of church and state in the United States has benefited both organized religion and American democracy. But that divide has always been a fuzzy one, and not everyone means the same thing when they speak of this separation. The concept of state goes beyond a particular political party or administration, and our understanding of God exceeds the bounds of organized religion.

There is a difference between church and state, and faith and politics. Faith motivates some people to seek public office, and faith certainly affects the way many people vote; these are Quadrant C, faith in daily life, expressions of faith. The Quadrant D, public ministry of the faith community, question is,

How can the church fulfill its prophetic mandate in a pluralistic society while also honoring the Constitutional separation of church and state and respecting the rights of others to hold different views? Such conversation itself is part of our precious heritage of religious freedom.

This session examines the dividing lines and the areas of overlap between church and state in the United States and explores the role, impact, and nuances of American civil religion. This information adds another layer to the foundation you and your study group are establishing so that as you pursue social justice ministry, you have a wider perspective and are better prepared to engage political and legal processes in your community and beyond.

Church and State Defined

Christians define the church in many ways, using rich metaphors such as the body of Christ, a royal priesthood, the household of God, a temple of living stones, and the new Israel. In this session, however, we use the legal definition from Internal Revenue Code 501(c) in which *church* is a shorthand reference to any voluntary association organized for religious purposes with a recognized creed, form and place of worship, and ecclesiastical government, such as a church, synagogue, temple, or mosque. (IRS Publication 1828, *Tax Guide for Churches and Religious Organizations,* lists 14 characteristics used to determine if an organization qualifies as a tax-exempt religious organization, but not all of these need to be satisfied.)

The U.S. Internal Revenue Code prohibits intervention in political campaigns by religious and other organizations as a condition for exemption from federal income tax under section 501(c)(3). (Much of the IRS-related material in this session comes from The Pew Forum on Religion and Public Life publication, *Politics and the Pulpit: A Guide to the Internal Revenue Code Restrictions on the Political Activity of Religious Organizations,* which is available online.)

State is a shorthand reference to the highest legally recognized civil authority within a defined geographical territory. It represents society acting as a whole - "We, the people" as stated in the Preamble to the U.S.

Constitution. The state holds the power to enforce its authority. The state's power, the Preamble goes on to say, is to "establish justice, insure domestic tranquility, provide for the common defense, promote the general welfare, and secure the blessings of liberty to ourselves and our posterity" and is legitimated by the Constitution. The concept of state embraces executive, legislative, and judicial powers exercised at all levels of government and thus includes programs, policies, and orders promulgated and enforced at national, state, and local levels.

Personal Reflection

When have you personally experienced tensions, questions, or doubts related to church and state relationships?

Historical Overview of Religious and Political Relationships

In biblical times

The Bible covers roughly 1900 years of history told first from the viewpoint of the Hebrew people who became the Israelites after they escaped from Egypt, and then from the perspectives of the earliest participants in the community formed around Jesus of Nazareth. What follows is a brief summary of the history and political circumstances surrounding these biblical "churches" and their relationship to the "emperor":

Abraham's migration from Ur into the land of Canaan where he and his descendants lived a semi-nomadic, clan-based existence is commonly dated to the 18th century BCE. Based on historical movements in the Fertile Crescent, it is likely that the tribe of Jacob was welcomed and prospered in Egypt during the next century while Egypt was under foreign control. The "rise of a new king over Egypt who did not know Joseph" (Ex 1:8) might have coincided with the restoration of Egyptian rule in the 16th century BCE. The once well-accepted Hebrew population in the Delta area was enslaved and oppressed until the time of the exodus, generally dated around 1290 BCE during the reign of Ramses II. In Egypt their experience of "God and emperor" was as voiceless slaves in a society in which the emperor (pharaoh) not only ruled economic and political affairs but was also understood to be a god.

Under Moses' leadership, these people came to know Yahweh as the one God of all history and creation who had liberated them from the Egyptians. Under Joshua, they settled in Canaan where they established a loose tribal confederacy from 1250-1030 BCE. The binding force among the twelve tribes was the covenant they shared under the kingship of Yahweh to whom they swore allegiance and whose laws they promised to keep. Religiously inspired tribal judges exercised occasional intertribal authority when necessitated by outside threats.

In response to growing Philistine successes against the tribes, a consolidated monarchy was established in 1030 BCE under the guidance of Samuel, the last judge of Israel. The Kingdom of Israel gained strength, territory, and recognition under kings Saul, David, and Solomon. As the power of the kings expanded, the great prophets of Israel arose to remind the kings that they too were subject to the laws of God and responsible for the wellbeing of their people. In this long period during which governance moved from tribal leaders to judges to kings, "God and emperor," though not one-in-the-same, were intimately connected by political and religious law.

Civil war broke out after Solomon's death in 922 BCE and the kingdom divided into the Southern (Judah) and Northern (Israel) kingdoms. The more prosperous Northern Kingdom fell to the Assyrians in 722/721 BCE. The Babylonians conquered Judah in 587 BCE and its leading citizens were exported to Babylon. The Babylonian exile extended from 587-538 BCE when King Cyrus of Persia, who had defeated the Babylonians, allowed the Jewish exiles to return to Jerusalem, rebuild the Temple, and develop their religious life under the tolerant political rule of Persia.

From this point through the time of the early church, except for one hundred years of independence following the Maccabean revolution in 167 BCE, the land of Israel was ruled by one foreign power after another - Assyria, Persia, Greece, and Rome. Once again the followers of Yahweh and, later, Jesus lived under a governance system that was not of their own making. Under some of these regimes, most notably the Persians, the Jews were free to follow their own religious beliefs and practices. At other times they suffered intense pressure to comply with prevailing cultural and religious customs, including emperor worship sporadically enforced by Rome against the first Christians.

The story of Daniel and the lion's den is perhaps the best-known Bible story of extended conflict between royal demands and faithful religious practice.

Because the early church rejected the prevailing religious practices of the Roman Empire and refused to offer sacrifices to the emperor, it was a persecuted minority for the first three hundred years of its existence. The Jewish people were largely tolerated in the Roman Empire, and this toleration had been extended to Christians, as long as they were viewed as a Jewish sect. When Christians were expelled from the synagogues following the Council of Jamnia in 90 CE, they lost this protection and were subject to sporadic but violent persecutions.

In 313 CE, Emperor Constantine issued the Edict of Milan that ended the persecution of Christians and restored confiscated property. Soon afterward, Christianity became the official religion of the Roman Empire, initiating the accommodation between church and state referred to as the Age of Christendom. In the mid-eleventh century (1054), the Eastern Church and the Roman Church separated. For the next five hundred years, the history of the Western world and the history of the Roman Catholic Church were closely intertwined, each having its ascendant moments in a variously cooperative and competitive relationship.

Church-state relationships in the age of Christendom

Here is a sampling of historical highlights and turning points:

Fifth century. After the collapse of the Roman Empire, the power of the church grew through its increasing influence in government, education, health, law, and art and its monopoly on "the keys to the kingdom of God," that is, the authority to forgive sin, which Jesus granted to the church via Peter and which was understood to give the church control over admission to heaven (Mt 16:19).

Eleventh century. The power struggle between popes and kings reached a climax in the dispute over control of appointments to church offices. King Henry IV deposed Pope Gregory VII, and the pope in turn excommunicated Henry. As tradition tells the story, the king stood three days waiting in the snow at Canossa to receive the pope's pardon.

Eleventh, twelfth, and thirteenth centuries. The Crusades wedded the church to the sword, totally intertwining ecclesiastical and secular power. This period, particularly during the reign of Pope Innocent III (1160-1216), represents the zenith of papal power.

The feudal system, in which kings were supported by surrounding lords and nobles, expanded royal bases of power. However, the relatively weakened church continued to be embroiled in political power struggles, including the Avignon Papacy created by the French king as a rival to Rome (1309-1377).

Sixteenth century. The Protestant Reformation challenged ecclesiastical power and abuses, ultimately dividing the Western church and weakening its power in relation to the state. Martin Luther criticized church practices and beliefs, particularly the sale of indulgences for the forgiveness of sin. John Calvin eliminated bishops and priests. King Henry VIII of England repudiated the power of Rome by establishing the Church of England. King James I of England proclaimed the divine right of kings as the basis for unquestioned obedience to his rule as did Louis XIV in France.

Sixteenth and seventeenth centuries. Religious and secular motives comingled in the intermittent wars of religion throughout Europe. The 1555 Peace of Augsburg established the principle that the faith of the king would decide the established faith of the kingdom. Both church and state were embroiled in the religious-based violence of the Counter-Reformation and Inquisition. The church used torture to obtain confessions and conversions and the state executed those condemned by the church.

Seventeenth century. The concept of separation of church and state emerged through the writings of John Locke, Charles de Montesquieu, and Jean Jacque Rousseau. These and other thinkers of that era provided the intellectual underpinnings for the rise of the modern state. Their writings deeply influenced the founding fathers of the United States and the framing of its Constitution.

Historical Models of Church and State

Though brief, the above timeline highlights the changing nature of the relationship between church and state throughout the history of the church. J. Philip Wogaman, in his book *Christian Perspectives on Politics,* identifies four different historical models: (1) *theocracy,* in which the state is controlled by religious leaders or institutions toward primarily religious ends; (2) *Erastianism,* named for the Swiss theologian, Thomas Erastus, in which political leadership uses and controls religion to increase the power of the state; *(3) friendly separation* of church and state in which separate but mutually respectful spheres of influence are legally regulated; and (4) *unfriendly separation* of church and state in which religion is discouraged, prohibited, or persecuted (p. 250).

Most of today's Western democracies have a "friendly separation" relationship between church and state; other types, however, existed during the colonial period of U.S. history. The Puritans who founded the Massachusetts Bay Colony in 1630 modeled a theocracy. Eight of the original thirteen colonies declared an established church, and every colony practiced some religious preferences such as tax benefits, clergy salaries, and religious tests for serving in the legislature. Catholics were not allowed to vote in Maryland, and Anglican Church attendance was required in the colony of Virginia. Roger Williams and Anne Hutchinson were banished from Massachusetts for their Quaker beliefs, and in 1660 Mary Dyer and other Massachusetts Quakers were executed. The founding fathers of the United States certainly had several models of a church-state relationship before them when they chose to include the principles of separation in the United States Constitution adopted in 1787 and the Bill of Rights adopted in 1791.

Even when the separation of church and state is "friendly" (Wogaman's third type), tensions still exist. In an essay addressing the principles of Catholic social teaching on the relationship between church and state, Clarke E. Cochran, in *Church, State and Public Justice: Five Views*, suggests that there is a constant shift and balance of four dynamics, depending upon the issue and the setting, namely: cooperation, challenge, competition, and transcendence (pp. 36-37). For example, the charity work of the church is typically done in *cooperation* with government social services. The 1983 Roman Catholic Bishops' pastoral letter on war and peace, *The Challenge of Peace: God's Promise and Our Response,* challenged policies of the U.S. Government. The 19th-century Catholic schools and orphanages were run in competition with state facilities. And the church understands that part of its mission *transcends* the "this world" role and purpose of the state.

Personal Reflection

What surprised you as you read this brief history? What insights did you gain?

The U.S. Constitution and Interpretations of Church and State

Separation between church and state continues to be a lively issue in American democracy. Some groups insist that separation is a myth never intended by the founding fathers. Other groups express alarm about what they see as encroachments that violate their understanding of the intended separation. (For example, see the WallBuilders website at www.wallbuilders. com and Americans United for Separation of Church and State at www.au.org.) The history surrounding the drafting of the Declaration of Independence and the U.S. Constitution includes a rich tapestry of opinions that are preserved in volumes of speeches, letters, and other documents. Each position can find ample "evidence" to support its position and refute that of others through careful selection of quotations and cases. *American Gospel: God, the Founding Fathers, and the Making of a Nation* by Jon Meacham offers a balanced, readable survey of U.S. church-state history.

Here is what the Constitution says about the relationship between church and state, along with some related observations and questions.

Articles, Amendments, and Cases

- **Article VI:** "No religious test shall ever be required as a qualification to any office or public trust under the United States."

While the legal standard is "no religious test," in practice there have always been de facto cultural tests. A Roman Catholic didn't have a prayer of being elected president before John F. Kennedy in 1960. In a speech to the Protestant Ministerial Association in Houston, he explicitly renounced any Catholic influence over the public exercise of his office. That renunciation was probably necessary for his election. During the primary season for the 2008 U.S. presidential election, Republican candidate Mitt Romney, a Mormon, found it necessary to give similar assurances. When

Rep. Keith Ellison, the first Muslim elected to U.S. Congress, took office in January 2007, there was a stir over his taking the oath of office on a copy of the Koran. Even today it's hard to imagine a declared atheist successfully running for U.S. president.

- **First Amendment:** "Congress shall make no law respecting an establishment of religion or prohibiting the free exercise thereof."

  Many of the most contentious court cases regarding church and state revolve around the delicate balance between "establishment" and "free exercise." When does accommodating the free expression of religious beliefs in publicly supported settings become promotion of religion, and when does maintaining neutrality become suppression? What is the difference between promoting a religious point of view and accurately reflecting a history replete with influential religious personalities and movements? Who can use public property for what purposes and under what circumstances?

- **Fourteenth Amendment, Section 1** (following the first sentence regarding citizenship): "No State shall make or enforce any law which shall abridge the privileges or immunities of citizens of the United States; nor shall any State deprive any person of life, liberty, or property, without due process of law; nor deny to any person within its jurisdiction the equal protection of the laws." (adopted in 1868)

  The Supreme Court has interpreted that, for the most part, the above due process and equal protection phrases of the Fourteenth Amendment extend the protections of the Constitution and the Bill of Rights not only to the Federal Government but also to the states. For example, the First Amendment always meant there could not be an established national church, but many states continued to financially support a particular denomination after the Constitution was ratified. Massachusetts did not abolish its established Congregational Church until 1833.

- **The Lemon Test:** One standard often cited by courts at all levels in deciding First Amendment cases concerning the constitutionality of a particular law is called the "Lemon Test," first articulated in a 1971 case, *Lemon v. Kurtzman.* To pass this three-pronged test, (1) the statute must have a secular legislative purpose; (2) the principal or primary effect of the statute must be one that neither advances nor inhibits religion; (3) the statute must not foster "an excessive entanglement with religion."

The Role of the Internal Revenue Service (IRS)

Within the confines of the above Constitutional provisions, the role of the public church, that is, how religious organizations can legally exert their influence on public policy, is largely governed by IRS codes for 501(c)(3) tax-exempt organizations. Some people have argued that any kind of tax exemption amounts to a government subsidy and therefore violates the establishment clause. Others insist that any tax and associated regulations violate the free exercise provision. The courts, however, have consistently upheld the constitutionality of regulating church political activity in return for tax-exempt status.

Here are some legal "do's and don'ts" for religious organizations regarding church political involvement based on *Politics and the Pulpit: A Guide to the Internal Revenue Code Restrictions on the Political Activity of Religious Organizations,* from the Pew Forum on Religion and Public Life. (Updates can be downloaded from http://pewforum.org/docs/ ?DocID=280.)

Do
- Discuss and promote issues of concern.
- Encourage members to register and vote.
- Sponsor candidate forums, giving equal access to all.
- Conduct voter education activities and distribute unbiased voter guides.
- Lobby legislators on behalf of issues (as a small part of overall mission).
- Keep personal political activity of clergy separate from the church.

Don't
- Do not endorse or oppose any candidate, party, or political action committee (PAC).
- Do not rate candidates.
- Do not provide or solicit financial or other support for a candidate, party, or PAC.

- Do not allow candidates to advertise or raise funds on church property.
- Do not distribute biased voter education guides or other materials.

It is both legal and appropriate for churches to reflect on the meaning of their faith in relation to public affairs and social justice and to engage wholeheartedly in the political process. As evident in recent years, various churches may have widely differing stances on some issues. Given this variety, it is important for all viewpoints to be openly represented in the public debate, consistent with applicable regulations, as part of the great concert of voices in our American democracy. The last session of the study will look further at how churches can do this.

Personal Reflection

1. How readily does your congregation engage in some of the "Do" activities listed on page 67?

2. When, if ever, have you observed religious groups engaging in any of the "Don't" activities (for example, endorsing a political candidate)? What was your reaction?

3. What is the difference between questioning the legality of a religious group's involvement and disagreeing with that group's position on an issue?

American Civil Religion

Historically, the "wall of separation" between church and state that Thomas Jefferson alluded to in his 1802 letter to the Danbury, Connecticut, Baptist Association has not existed. Later observers have used more accurate metaphors such as a "picket fence" or a "veil of separation" because our nation's history and public life are filled with religious references and overtones.

In answer to the question, "What is America?" G. K. Chesterton once described the United States as "a nation with the soul of a church." U.S. presidents freely invoke the name of God in speeches and sometimes in public prayers. The phrase "under God" is on U.S. coins and was added to the Pledge of Allegiance in 1954. Religious chaplains serve legislative bodies and the armed forces. Such practices represent a cluster of customs, beliefs, and values often referred to as America's civil religion. The classic definition of civil or public religion comes from a 1967 article "Civil Religion in America" by sociologist Robert Bellah:

> Although matters of personal religious belief, worship, and association are considered to be strictly private affairs, there are, at the same time, certain common elements of religious orientation that the great majority of Americans share. These have played a crucial role in the development of American institutions and still provide a religious dimension for the whole fabric of American life, including the political sphere. This public religious dimension is expressed in a set of beliefs, symbols, and rituals that I am calling American civil religion (reprinted in *American Civil Religion*, p. 24).

Civil religion is a secular, widely accepted tradition prevalent in American history and society that might appear to violate the separation of church and state. Largely ceremonial and non-creedal, it provides a transcendent aura to American public life and invokes God's blessing on this country and its endeavors without articulating specific beliefs and expectations. The Declaration of Independence, for example, uses the titles Nature's God, Divine Providence, and Creator to attach a general sense of divine inspiration to the actions being taken.

Many of the entities of U.S. civil religion evoke a reverence similar to religious symbols and artifacts. As suggested by the list below, they provide common references that unite Americans in the same way their religious counterparts unite faith communities.

1. **Sacred texts:** Declaration of Independence, President Lincoln's Gettysburg Address

2. **Symbols:** U.S. flag, Statue of Liberty

3. **Saints:** George Washington, Abraham Lincoln, Rosa Parks

4. **Shrines:** Lincoln Memorial, Mount Rushmore, Washington Monument, the 9/11 Memorial at Ground Zero

5. **Holy Days:** Fourth of July, Memorial Day, Thanksgiving Day

6. **Hymns:** "America the Beautiful," "God Bless America," "The Star Spangled Banner"

7. **Martyrs**: Abraham Lincoln, John F. Kennedy, Martin Luther King Jr.

In civil religion, God's will is typically linked to freedom and democracy rather than to more specifically Christian themes such as hope, repentance, redemption, reconciliation, and salvation. At its best, American civil religion has been a unifying factor reflecting widely shared values and reinforcing generally recognized moral standards. In more recent years, as the United States has become increasingly diverse, more objections are being raised about what used to be routine practices, such as the National Day of Prayer, invocations at public functions, and government-sponsored Christmas displays. In response to such objections, some conservative Christians now talk about the government's "war on Christmas" and the persecution of Christianity in the United States.

Civil religion is subject to dangerous misuse. It readily acculturates into a cozy blessing of the status quo. When national symbols take on religious overtones, the result can be a form of patriotism that risks morphing into idolatry of nation. It is important for American Christians to be aware of this possible syncretism so that our ability to critique the systems, institutions, and practices of our own country through the lens of biblical justice and the gospel of Christ is not compromised.

In his book *Being Christian in an Almost Chosen Nation: Thinking about Faith and Politics,* H. Stephen Shoemaker describes the two-edged sword of civil religion: "The promise of civil religion is its belief that we can be about the work of God in history. Such belief has given us the moral vision and moral energy to defeat tyranny, establish democracy, end slavery, and grant women political equality. The peril of civil religion is that it can lead a nation to claim too much, to self-righteousness, and to a blindness to its own human weaknesses" (p. 24-25).

Acknowledging the inevitability of American civil religion, church scholar Diana Butler Bass asks these important questions in her book *Broken We Kneel: Reflections on Faith and Citizenship:* "The question is not whether we will have civil religion; rather, the question is: what sort of civil religion will we have? ... Will America's emerging civil religion be priestly or prophetic? Militant or realistic? Exclusive or ecumenical?" (p. 8).

These are challenging questions that should concern all Americans, particularly Christians, since Christianity has been the primary shaper of this public religion. The dangers of civil religion addressed in this section certainly should not preclude love of country and appreciation for the freedoms U.S. citizens enjoy. They do, however, caution us to be aware of these dynamics as part of our thoughtful exploration of public goals and policies and our honest, faith-based critique of systemic injustices and abuses of power.

Personal Reflection

Why do you think the issue of civil religion is addressed in this study? What is your reaction to the subject?

Discerning the Dividing Line

Throughout this study you and others in your congregation have examined why the church needs to be engaged in all four arenas of faith expression, discussed how to recognize and overcome resistance to social justice ministry, gained appreciation for the impact of social location and how it limits our awareness, and learned new communication skills. This session has focused on recognizing the "picket fence" or "veil" that separates church and state so that your congregation can pursue its prophetic mandate while respecting the rights of others who hold different views. The next session builds on "preparing the soil" for social justice ministry by examining healthy and unhealthy conflict behaviors and skills for communicating in a conflicted situation.

Session Six
Beyond Avoidance: Healthy Conflict is Possible

My friend Rita was bemoaning the fact that her church had not paid any attention to a denominational conference appeal on behalf of neighboring immigrant families who had been disrupted by an INS (Immigration and Naturalization Service) raid and subsequent deportations. When I asked what she had tried to do about it, she replied, "Well I didn't want to say anything because it's a controversial subject in our community." I knew Rita had strong feelings about immigrant rights and that she had learned a lot about the needs and conditions of the migrant workers whose labor enables the summer crops of our state to be harvested. She was not comfortable, however, bringing up their plight in church because she knew there were differing opinions about the presence of the immigrants and what the government's policies should be. It turned out that the minister had wanted to lift up the denominational appeal but he, too, was reluctant "to stir up a storm in the church."

Both Rita and her minister were exhibiting a fear of conflict that is rampant in many churches. This fear is based on the false assumption that Christians should not have differences and that any conflict is a bad thing for the church. In her book *Leaving Church,* Barbara Brown Taylor observes, "Because church people tend to think they should not fight, most of them are really bad at it"(p. 109). In fact, as attested in the apostle Paul's letters, conflict has been an integral part of the church since its earliest beginnings. As noted in *Moving Your Church through Conflict* by church consultant Speed Leas, "Conflict over whether the church should be involved in social issues, or which side the church should take on such issues, has been with us since Jesus challenged the dietary laws of the Sadducees and Pharisees" (p. 101).

This session focuses on readying yourself and your church to deal with conflict as you become intentional about social justice ministry. Learning to recognize healthy and unhealthy conflict behaviors and ways to communicate in conflicted situations are essential relational skills.

Conflict Is Inevitable

Conflict - differing perceptions, opinions, feelings, wants, needs, goals, and priorities - is an inevitable part of all human relationships and organizations. Each person is unique; each of us has differing experiences and social locations. The real issue is not whether there will be conflict but rather how conflict is perceived and addressed.

The costs of repressed conflict are steep. People tiptoe around each other, fostering superficial relationships. Resentments build up and misunderstandings fester. Their repression leads to antagonism and reactive behaviors that seem to come out of nowhere. In the case above, Rita was frustrated, angry, and disappointed with her church. She stopped attending and ultimately resigned, which shocked and dismayed other church members.

In the name of conflict avoidance, the church missed an opportunity to learn more about some neighbors in need. The minister and others in the congregation who might have shared Rita's concerns remained isolated from one another. The hardships experienced by the immigrants continued. Manipulative, questionable employment practices went unchallenged. As the prophet Jeremiah said, lamenting the failure of his community to address the great issues of his time, "They have treated the wound of my people carelessly, saying, 'Peace, peace,' when there is no peace" (Jer 6:14; 8:11). When we fail to be fully engaged in the world and with one another, the whole body of Christ is diminished.

When a church community intentionally confronts controversial issues rather than avoids them, a different, potentially life-giving dynamic comes into play. Confidence displaces the fear of conflict. Shared learning promotes individual and communal growth. Careful, respectful listening increases mutual trust and knowledge. We find we can be agreeable in our disagreements. In the delightful words of one parishioner who often disagreed with me, "If you and I agreed on everything, one of us wouldn't be needed." As the capacity of the congregation to deal with differences expands, the church can become a model for conflict resolution and healing in the fractured world outside the church. This is truly being a "city set on a hill" for all to see (Mt 5:14 rsv).

In his foreword to Speed Leas's *Moving Your Church through Conflict,* Loren Mead from The Alban Institute writes:

> We have learned that the fullest life is the life that goes beyond cheap peace to a peace that indeed far surpasses our understanding and our dreams. It is a peace that includes the broadest varieties, the strongest differences. That kind of peace is like the richest of polyphonic harmonies, blending a rich diversity into a complex, tension-filled unity, far beyond uniformity (p. 4).

Personal Reflection

1. What is your attitude about conflict? From where or what do you think that attitude originates? For example, I find conflict unpleasant and try to avoid it because that was the pattern in my family. I therefore had no positive examples of healthy, productive conflict.

2. What do you think is the attitude of your congregation as a whole toward conflict?

Deadly Conflict Behaviors

The widespread propensity to avoid conflict typically stems from painful experiences marked by unhealthy conflict behaviors. Due to the prevalence of negative behaviors in conflicted situations and the scarcity of positive examples, it's no wonder people tend to equate conflict itself with the damage caused by the hurtful behaviors. The unhealthy behaviors described in this section, often exhibited during times of conflict, are offered not as an exhaustive list of such behaviors but rather as reminders to help you discern the health of your own and others' behavior in times of conflict.

Fear-based behaviors

As previously mentioned, the fear of controversy promotes conflict avoidance. Fear of personal rejection inhibits honest expression, which distorts a healthy conflict process. If we think we are supposed to know everything, we will fear exposure and be reluctant to ask questions. Fear of losing face often lies behind an inability to compromise, negotiate, or let go. One's own sense of inadequacy may be at the root of aggressive behavior such as labeling, threatening, belittling, or dismissing others. This type of behavior unnecessarily escalates the level of a conflict and obscures meaningful collaboration to reach good public policy solutions.

Indirect generalizations

In the attempt to bolster a position, we make indirect generalizations - sweeping, unverifiable claims about what "everyone" is saying or what "people" are thinking or doing. (Children learn this technique at an early age.) The "everyone" gambit is also a way to avoid taking responsibility for our own opinions and having to explain them. It impedes honest communication and exploration of ideas since those "others" are never present to engage in the process.

Rumors, gossip, and secrets

Rumors, gossip, and secrets are utterly antithetical to the Spirit of Christ and destructive to any community. They foster divisiveness and mistrust. Rumors and gossip are used to discredit opponents in a conflict. They shift attention away from the issues and ideas that need to be addressed. Secrets and closed-door meetings create insiders and outsiders. Often their intent is to force a particular outcome by short-circuiting a full, open process.

Side-stepping defined structures and process

All churches have designated leaders, committees, and some kind of decision-making process. These are usually outlined in bylaws, covenants, charters, or other approved documents. While it is true that a bureaucratic atmosphere can have a deadening effect on churches, it is imperative in times of conflict to have and follow recognized areas of responsibility and authority - not to impose control but to facilitate open engagement.

Distortions of the truth

People involved in conflict are tempted to distort the facts in order to win others to their "side." We may exaggerate or omit pertinent data that doesn't support our case. We become more concerned with winning an argument than with resolving the conflict in the best interests of all those affected. Selective case building retards the knowledge base of the group and muddies the credibility of the proponents. This is what all of us are doing, whether we are conscious of it or not, when we limit our information sources by consulting only the friends we intuitively know will agree with us; by tuning into only "friendly" radio stations and TV channels; and by reading only the newspapers, columnists, magazines, and websites that reflect our viewpoints.

Closed-mindedness

Close-mindedness recalls the false sense of certitude explored in the Session 3 discussion about social location and designed blindness. When people enter a conflicted situation convinced that their position is 100 percent right and therefore anyone differing with them is just plain wrong, constructive conflict is impossible. No learning or growth or change will occur, and the community suffers.

Creating "straw men"

Sadly, politicians of every persuasion all too often model the subtle skill of redefining the issue at hand to create an easily dismissed position rather than tackling the real, more challenging or complex problem at hand. Step 4 of the 12-Step Alcoholics Anonymous program is to make "a searching and fearless moral inventory of ourselves." The best antidote I know for the temptation to create straw men is the call for "searching and fearless" honesty.

Bullying

Bullying includes psychological force such as manipulation, blaming, shouting, intimidating, and threatening to pull out of an activity. Others may placate the bully simply to get rid of the unpleasant behavior. This, of course, rewards that behavior and increases the likelihood of its being repeated. Even monopolizing a conversation can be a mild form of bullying.

Win-lose mentality

When a conflict polarizes into factions, it takes on the aura of a contest rather than a shared search for resolution. Each camp goes about its own business of searching for votes and convincing the "undecideds." There may be phone calls, letters, emails, and visits to bring in new players. The "winners" are more apt to celebrate their victory than to express concern for the inclusion and healing of the "losers," that is, those whose will or hopes were not realized. Paul's description of the church as a place where, when one suffers, all suffer, is effaced (1 Cor 12:26).

Personal Reflection

Recall a painful church conflict that you experienced or have heard about:

1. Which of the unhealthy behaviors described, or other unhealthy behaviors, were associated with that conflict?

2. What was the aftermath of this conflict?

3. In hindsight, what might the various participants in the conflict have done
   differently?

4. The 2016 presidential election was one of the most negative campaigns in
recent history. What deadly conflict behaviors did you observe?

Healthy Conflict Behaviors

Conflict is as inevitable in the church as in any other community. Our
calling, as suggested in the apostle Paul's introductory words to his great
passage in 1 Corinthians 13, is to find "a still more excellent way" (12:31).
Paul describes a way that is patient, loving, and kind. It is not envious,
boastful, or arrogant; it does not insist on its own way and is not irritable or
resentful; it rejoices not in wrongdoing but in the truth.

Here are some behaviors widely recommended by conflict management
consultants and marriage counselors that can foster the more excellent way
Paul describes. This pattern of relating to one another is effective in all
situations, but is particularly valuable in times of conflict.

Deal directly with the parties involved

Don't talk about people and your differences with them behind their backs. This type of communication is often called triangulation because it may be an attempt to communicate with a person through a third party. And sometimes people do it to justify themselves without having to deal with opposing viewpoints. Talking about disagreements face to face feels risky. But when people only talk to people who share the same point of view, nothing is accomplished. Direct confrontation becomes easier the more widely it is practiced and accepted as the norm of the community.

Define what the issue, problem, or difference is

Occasionally conflicts can be resolved when the affected parties gather simply to acknowledge the tension and work together to clarify what the issues or areas of difference actually are. If significant differences are still clearly present, they can then design a process to follow for addressing them. This affirms the underlying relationships and encourages ownership of the process.

Be informed

Seek more information about the conflict issue and related background data, including the polity and positions of your church. Check out sources when rumors are floating around. Be open to other perspectives and experiences. Again, using a variety of sources, including those that do not support your own opinions, provides greater balance and will help you see more clearly where others are coming from. In the spirit of the well-known prayer of St. Francis, seek to understand at least as well as you seek to be understood.

Speak for yourself

Use "I" language, as in "I think," "I saw," "I wish," or "This passage in the Bible means this to me." *"I"* language avoids the unhealthy "people are saying" kind of generalizations mentioned in the preceding section on unhealthy conflict behaviors. It pushes us to take responsibility for honestly expressing ourselves without trying to speak for someone else or putting others on the defensive. Speaking our truth with love is always the goal.

Listen respectfully to others

Review the listening skills discussed in Session 3, "Opening Ourselves to the Gifts of Others." Think of listening as a form of love. Focus on ideas without judging the motives or intelligence of those who disagree with you. Especially in a conflicted situation, tension is defused when you paraphrase the speaker's opinions in your own words to be sure you have correctly understood them even when you don't agree with them. Hopefully, your grace-filled effort will be reciprocated.

Practice creative problem solving

Because so many people are uncomfortable with conflict, we may be tempted to latch onto any proposal just to put an issue to rest. This gives an undue advantage to whoever speaks up first or loudest. Brainstorming is an excellent way to get more people involved, share responsibility for handling conflict, and prevent premature conclusions. The secret for good brainstorming is to encourage participants to speak freely without self-censoring their thoughts and to openly record all ideas without discussion until everyone is satisfied. The group may then evaluate the suggestions and build a plan.

Distinguish between opinions and personhood

Keep the conflict focused on issues. Even as you disagree strongly with someone's idea or action, try to express your care and concern for that person. Refrain from personal attacks, character assassination, and questioning another's motives. This is important in all circumstances, but particularly in the church where we are called to cultivate the Spirit of Christ.

Keep your perspective

Maintain a sense of humor; lighten up and accept the possibility that your thinking can change. Look for areas of agreement such as shared values and goals. Continue to participate in worship, ministries, and programs apart from the conflict. Remember that in the history of the church, people have separated, fought, and even killed one another over issues that had no lasting significance.

Personal Reflection

Recall an example of healthy conflict you have been part of or observed.
What factors and behaviors contributed to its success?

Spiritual Resources for Ministries of Reconciliation

The above described strategies and behaviors apply in both secular and
religious settings. The followers of Jesus Christ, however, and the church
called to be the Body of Christ in the world have additional spiritual
resources and motivation for addressing important but controversial issues.
Jesus said, "You will know the truth, and the truth will make you free" (John
8:32). Jesus was talking not about truth as factual knowledge but truth as a
way of life imbued by God's Spirit and committed to Christ. Surely those
who seek the fullness of this way and the freedom it promises cannot be
governed by fear of conflict or allow themselves to be satisfied with easy
answers.

The apostle Paul reminded the conflicted church in Corinth that
reconciliation was the purpose of Christ's ministry. God was in Christ
reconciling the world to its creator; those who are in Christ are given that
ministry of reconciliation. We become, in Paul's words, "ambassadors for
Christ" (2 Cor 5:16-20). All this is part of becoming God's new creation.
Surely this is a calling for the church to be boldly engaged in all aspects of
life, seeking and serving the common good in the midst of divergent
understandings of what that should look like.

The command to love one another - not just those who agree with us, but
our perceived adversaries as well - adds a deeper dimension to the healthy
conflict behaviors suggested above. "Bless those who persecute you; bless
and do not curse them" (Rom 12:14). It's hard to pray for those with whom

we are in conflict. We may want God to just change their minds or get them out of our way, but this is a prayer for ourselves, not for them. In the words of Marjorie Thompson in her book *Soul Feast,* "Prayer is participation in willing God's will" (p. 41). The safest way to pray for an enemy is simply to imagine them being bathed in God's love or "holding them in the light," as the Quakers might say. It's amazing how this practice changes one's own attitude toward another person or group.

Jesus' prayer "that they may all be one" does not mean everyone has to think alike. It does compel us to make our churches safe places for people to explore ideas, debate policies, and express disagreement in loving and respectful ways. We must create hospitable environments where conflict is expected, prepared for, and handled with confidence, humility, and grace. If the followers of Jesus Christ, the Prince of Peace, cannot deal with their differences in constructive ways, how can we expect the nations of the world to do so?

Personal Reflection

Try praying regularly, perhaps for seven days, for someone with whom you are in conflict and record how that feels here:

A Conflict Story: Where Does the Flag Belong?

When I became the pastor of a midsized church in Minnesota, I brought with me the assumption that the display of national flags in a sanctuary where we worship the God of all nations is inappropriate. I don't recall asking anyone about the church's own history and expectations about that; somewhere along the way, I simply moved the U.S. flag and a Christian flag out into the narthex. The flags were regularly displayed in church on the Sunday closest to the Fourth of July and whenever the assigned altar guild person decided to put them out. On those Sundays I would typically hear a few comments that "it was nice to see the flag in church this morning." If the flags overstayed their welcome, in my opinion, I took them out. I had no idea how strongly many people felt about having the flags in the sanctuary because it was never discussed.

A strongly worded email responding to an off-hand sermon comment prompted me to ask the chair of the Board of Deacons to call a special meeting to discuss what members were thinking and feeling about the flag-in-the-sanctuary issue. On the appointed Sunday, I entered the meeting room expecting to find the five or six people that I knew had strong feelings about having the flag in the sanctuary. Almost ten times that number had gathered.

The deacon chair laid out some ground rules: (1) Each person would have a chance to speak to the issue. (2) Only one person would speak at a time. (3) There would be no discussion or response to any speaker. (4) Anyone could pass if they chose not to speak. Then we spent more than two hours listening to each person share their thoughts and feelings about the flag issue. We heard many viewpoints and personal stories. No one responded or commented on anything that was said. We simply listened to every speaker. It was a moving and powerful experience that affected us all.

At the end of our time together, I think we felt a deepened sense of appreciation for every person there, which trumped the importance of seeing our own viewpoint prevail. No one wanted to have a vote. We asked the Board of Deacons to decide on a policy, which they did. The policy was to bring both flags into the sanctuary on the Sunday nearest designated civic holidays with the reason printed in the bulletin along with a related prayer suggestion. At other times the flags stood in the vestibule near the entrance of the sanctuary. A year later the policy was amended to also welcome the flags in the sanctuary on any Sunday when it was requested by a member, with the name of the requester and reason printed in the bulletin.

We learned a lot as a result of the flag controversy in that church. I learned that this kind of decision belongs to the whole church, not the pastor. We grew in our willingness to address a controversial issue and to trust an agreed-upon process. We saw that some things are even more important than our own opinions. We didn't do it perfectly. I suspect there were some eyes rolling upward now and then and some folks thought the summary of the meeting printed in the church newsletter was a little slanted, but many of the healthy behaviors identified in this session were clearly being practiced and that made a significant difference.

Personal Reflection

1. Recall a time when understanding why someone feels differently than you do about an important issue has helped you accept them and respect their viewpoint despite your differences.

2. What additional thoughts or questions would you add to this session?

Speaking the Truth in Love

Conflict is inevitable in all human relationships and will arise as you and your congregation pursue social justice activities. Christians are called to engage our honest differences with one another in healthy ways, which ultimately can serve God's desire for justice and unity. Our final session will discuss strategies and will practice a process for undertaking the next steps.

Session Seven
Strengthening our Congregation's Public Witness

Effective social justice ministry is not compartmentalized and delegated to a small number of participants. Rather, it is integrated into every part of the church's program and ministry: worship, preaching, study, education, Christian formation, pastoral care, outreach, and evangelism. We do not need to choose between being a prophetic church or a pastoral church, between responding to immediate needs of people or advocating long-term structural changes in our social institutions, or between personal faith and public action, because these are all false polarities. While certain boards, committees, ministry teams, lay leaders, and staff members may have particular responsibilities that relate more closely to one of these areas, social justice ministry is an integral part of every aspect of a congregation's ministry because God's love and justice embrace all of life.

Theologian Harvey Cox, in his book *Religion in a Secular City,* describes the church as God's pervasive presence in the world, quoting Ignacio Ellacuria in *Freedom Made Flesh:* "The presence of God in the world cannot simply be proclaimed, it must be made visible; it must be mediated and fleshed out. The church must be the tangible sign of God's presence" (p. 102). What does that presence look like now? What will that presence look like in the future? How does your congregation give God's presence form now? In the weeks, months, and years to come, how will your church give it form and manifest it in the world? How does a faith community reflect, plan, prioritize, act, and learn together to advocate social justice? What kind of ministry will best serve the needs of the community and enrich the lives of all those involved?

This final session identifies the critical elements for effective social justice ministry in a congregation and will help you begin to plan the next steps for the public witness of your congregation.

Elements of Effective Social Justice Ministry

Although every church will have its own approach, goals, and priorities for social justice ministry, the following elements are an essential part of any successful church program:

- A spiritual foundation
- Leadership and organization
- Education
- A focus
- Strategic analysis and planning
- Connection and collaboration
- Communication and publicity
- Ownership

A Spiritual Foundation

Nurturing the spiritual foundations for social justice ministry is critical. The foundations for the church's public witness must be deeply rooted in the faith and traditions of the congregation to avoid being defined and shaped by cultural values and norms, partisan politics, or the governing authorities ("emperor"). Its spiritual roots distinguish the church's social justice ministry from that of secular groups. Prayer, study, worship, and ongoing Christian formation direct and sustain all ministries of the church. Social justice ministry is spiritually enriched by effective preaching and by Bible study, often based on one of the explicitly prophetic books of the Bible. The following resources may be especially helpful to mainline Protestant churches rediscovering their traditional spiritual roots and practices:

Soul Feast: An Invitation to the Christian Spiritual Life by Marjorie Thompson

Christianity for the Rest of Us: How the Neighborhood Church Is Transforming the Faith by Diana Butler Bass

The Practicing Congregation: Imagining a New Old Church by Diana Butler Bass

Changing the Conversation: A Third Way for Congregations by Anthony B. Robinson

Leadership and Organization

Leadership is key for successful social justice ministry. To promote imaginative vision, reliable interpretation, and widespread support for social justice efforts, lay leaders must understand its importance, scope, and relationship to everything the church does. Clergy leadership and commitment are essential for articulating a faith that compels the congregation's engagement in social justice ministry; for recruiting, equipping, and empowering strong lay leadership; and for promoting sensitivity to social justice issues in every aspect of the congregation's life and ministry.

While various parts of the church will be involved in different ways and to varying levels of intensity, designating a locus of responsibility is critical for promoting and coordinating social justice ministry in the formal organizational structure of the congregation. Typically, this might be a social action committee or mission and outreach board. Some churches combine the two Quadrant D functions of charity and justice in the same group, while others separate them. However, unless the distinction between these two parts of Quadrant D are clearly addressed, social justice ministry often gets short shrift when the functions are combined in one committee.

Education

As has been emphasized throughout this study, social justice and the church's calling to be engaged in that part of the church's public ministry must be an integral part of congregational life, particularly in its formal education program: Sunday school - youth and adult - including curricula materials, speakers, book studies, special programs, field trips, and so forth. Other ideas will become apparent as you read this final session and during the closing session of your group study. But be patient. It's important to have specific educational objectives but also to spread them over enough time so that your resources are not overwhelmed, potential participants are not burned out, and study topics have time to be digested and acted upon. It's better to let the learning and energy from one study, such as this one, spread wider and deeper throughout the congregation than to move too quickly to something else.

A Focus

In a world where we are surrounded by endless needs and issues, it is easy to become paralyzed. While the church cares about all of these issues, each local faith community must focus its attention and energy on specific, tangible goals. A well-known parable tells of a child who walked along the beach throwing dehydrated starfish back into the ocean. A skeptical bystander pointed out that the shore was lined with countless thousands of dying starfish and asked what difference her actions could possibly make. The child leaned over to pick up another starfish and toss it into the water. "It makes a difference to this one," she said.

While the church cares about all the starfish - the needs, injustices, and issues of the day - we will grow more in our capacity to serve God in the world through specific, in-depth engagement in one or two clearly defined areas rather than constructing positions and pronouncements on every possible public concern. We can trust that other parts of the larger body of Christ in the world will be called to pick up other starfish.

Strategic Analysis and Planning

When Jesus sent his disciples out into the world, he told them to "be wise as serpents and innocent as doves" (Mt 10:16). He advised his followers to plan realistically and budget wisely to insure the success of their commitments (Lk 14:25-32). From among all the needs and justice issues facing our society, how is a local church to decide where to focus its outreach and resources? How can you possibly get a handle on such complicated issues when there are often contradictory perspectives and competing remedies?

The best way to encourage independent, faith-based thinking in the congregation about social justice issues is to develop skills in social analysis. A widely used resource for this is the book *Social Analysis: Linking Faith and Justice*. Its authors, Joe Holland and Peter Henriot, begin with the premise that congregations need to become engaged with the lived experience of people to learn firsthand what is going on in their communities. After inserting themselves into the setting through projects, interviews, and visits, participants ask questions, such as these below, to discern possible social justice issues and appropriate responses:

- What are some significant needs in this community?
- What unique gifts do we as a church have to offer in this situation?
- How does this situation affect people on the margins of society?
- How is economic power being employed in this situation?
- What are the costs of inaction, and what segments of society are paying those costs?
- What do we want to accomplish by engaging in this issue or situation?

Based on this kind of social analysis, along with theological reflection through the lens of the gospel and Christian tradition, your church might select one need or issue to focus on. It would then plan and carry out a response, evaluate the results of the action taken, and use the evaluation for future planning and program modification. The development of this circular pattern of action and reflection over time is invaluable to the public ministry (Quadrant D) of a congregation.

Connection and Collaboration

Be on the alert for congregation members with interests and experiences gained in Quadrants A, B, C, and the social outreach side of D who can also strengthen and serve the social justice side of Quadrant D. For example, a member's Quadrant C volunteer work could grow into a church-wide advocacy effort as more members join the effort, learn about the needs, and talk about why these needs are growing. Or the largely Quadrant B-oriented worship committee of a predominantly white church might plan a joint worship service for Martin Luther King Day with a nearby, predominantly African American church. It begins as a largely symbolic undertaking, but friendships formed during the planning process reveal common concerns for local school funding that draw the previously complacent white church into advocacy.

Carl Dudley, sociologist and professor at Hartford Seminary, highlights the importance of bridge people who help a congregation connect to groups whose interests it is seeking to serve. When there are cultural, economic, racial, educational, or geographic differences between the congregation and the group to be served, it is immensely helpful to have someone with a foot in both camps to help introduce and interpret one group to another. Another way churches get started in new kinds of ministries is through joining with another congregation already engaged in that ministry or by modeling what other churches have done.

In a pluralistic democracy, the church enters the public square as an equal player with all other interests and viewpoints. The church translates its faith-based policies and positions into broadly based civic values and virtues to foster honest dialogue in a pluralistic setting. That is, in seeking to influence public policy, Christians of all stripes will work with one another, with people of other faiths, and with people of no faith to structure life together for the common good.

Communication and Publicity

Communication is the lifeblood of any congregation. It is particularly important for moving social justice ministry from the margins into the mainstream of congregational life. How do members and friends find out what's going on and who's doing what? How are visitors and guests informed about the congregation's public ministry and invited to get involved? How can everyone learn from the experiences of a few? How will the experience of this study group be shared with the wider congregation?

Typical outlets for such communication include newsletters, bulletin boards, pamphlets, bulletin inserts, Sunday morning announcements, educational forums, and word of mouth. An increasing number of churches now also have websites, Facebook pages, email lists, and interest blogs. For strengthening social justice ministry in the local church, it's important for communications to be regular and identifiable as social justice ministry, such as having a designated web page, a column in the newsletter, a logo or slogan, or regular social justice Sundays on the church calendar.

Ownership

In our high-tech world, we are besieged by information, requests for support, and calls for action from many valid and worthy entities. Denominational offices and interest groups issue pronouncements and positions on so many issues that average people in the pews get overwhelmed and turned off. We may sign our name onto an emailed petition, but we may not have enough ownership in or commitment to that cause for it to affect our lives and faith at a meaningful level. While this kind of distanced response has a place, it is no substitute for personal engagement in specific ways with head, heart, spirit, hands, pocketbook, time, and talents. Doing this with others in a faith community adds further grounding, reflection, hope, and joy to the endeavor and, over time, transforms the congregation itself.

Ownership is strengthened through incremental steps and commitments, such as when a member decides to post a story or need on the social action bulletin board or asks permission to circulate a petition in the congregation or invites a friend involved with prison reform to speak to a Sunday school class. Before any decision to use church funds or to publicly advocate on behalf of a specific issue, group, bill, action, or boycott is made, do good research and offer educational opportunities, provide open discussion and debate, and have the congregation vote. The very act of defining such a process helps to increase congregational awareness of social justice ministry and broaden the church's commitment and expectations.

Assessing the Presence and Strength of Key Elements

Like all other endeavors, a church seeking to extend its social justice ministry begins where it is. Building on its own history, strengths, and existing links and relationships can help a congregation sharpen its focus and move forward. The following survey is intended to help you do this, first individually and then together as a group during this final session of the study.

Individual Assessment Survey

Think about the questions below, making notes as you go along. At the end of each section rate your congregation using a 1 to 10 scale, with 1 being the weakest score and 10 being the strongest. Do not worry about being too precise--this is a rather subjective assessment. You will be invited to combine your totals with those of other participants to reach a composite "score."

A. Spiritual Foundations:

1. How often do you see your faith explicitly affecting your stance on a question of public policy?

2. How comfortable do you think members of your church are in talking about their faith and other spiritual matters?

3. Where do you see and experience links between spirituality and social justice in your church?

Your rating (1-10): _____

B. Leadership and Organization:

1. Is there a focal point (person or group) for social justice ministry in your church and how well integrated is this focal point into the formal organization and lifeblood of the church?

2. How clearly is the distinction between the charity and the social justice components of public ministry (Quadrant D) reflected in the organization and mindset of the congregation?

3. How strong, as you see it, is your pastor's commitment to the social justice part of Quadrant D public ministry?

Your rating (1-10): _____

C. Education:

1. How would you rate the social justice consciousness of your church's education program in the Sunday school?   Youth Programming?   Adult Education?

2. What percentage of the adult congregation engages in Sunday or midweek adult education opportunities?

3. Where do you see intentional theological reflection related to current events and issues taking place in the life of your church?

Your rating (1-10): _____

D. Focus

1. How are local, state, national, and global issues addressed in the church community? Which ones get the most attention?

2. Would most members be able to name one or two social justice related issues that your church is engaged in?

3. How engaged in social justice do you think people in other churches and in the wider community see your church?

Your rating (1-10): _____

E. Strategic Analysis and Planning

1. How clearly defined and understood are the objectives for the outreach your church is doing?

2. When does evaluation of church initiatives and programs take place?

3. How thoroughly are such evaluations performed and communicated?

Your rating (1-10): _____

F. Connections and Collaboration

1. Where do you see evidence of crossover among the quadrants in the life of your church?

2. How many potential "bridge people" can you identify in the congregation?

3. How connected is your church to denominational and ecumenical advocacy groups, regional or national?

Your rating (1-10): _____

G. Communications and Publicity:

1. How evident are the church's social justice concerns in a typical newsletter and/or the church's website if you have one?

2. What existing outlets are available for reporting on the experience of this study, and how readily would you use them?

Your rating (1-10): _____

H. Ownership:

1. What percentage of the church's active membership is engaged in the Quadrant D life of the church?

2. What is the level of your personal commitment to seeing your church become more engaged in social justice advocacy?

Your rating (1-10): _____

Add the eight ratings to get your total readiness score: _____

Personal Reflection

Take a few minutes to review this Participant Book, thinking about what has been covered, what issues have come up for you, and what you want for your church with regard to its social justice ministry.

1. What is something you are thankful for?

2. What is one new insight or learning you gained in this study?

3. What is a hope you have for social justice ministry in your church?

4. What is one thing you will do in the next month as a result of this study?

Concluding Words

In a July 5,1965, speech to Fifth Synod of the United Church of Christ, Dr. Martin Luther King Jr. said: "Although the Church has been called to combat social evils, it has often remained silent behind the anesthetizing security of stained glass windows . . . How often the Church has been an echo rather than a voice, a taillight behind the Supreme Court and other secular agencies, rather than a headlight guiding men and women progressively and decisively to higher level of understanding."

The Christian community is enriched and the lives of people inside and outside the church are transformed as they work together to inquire about, seek, and find just resolutions to social inequities. We grow in understanding and love as we live out our faith together and as we develop increased confidence and skills. "Let your light shine before others," Jesus said, "so that they may see your good works and give glory to [God]" (Mt 5:16). This is indeed the work of the kin-dom we are called to seek and to serve.

"Never doubt that a small group of thoughtful, committed, citizens can change the world. Indeed, it is the only thing that ever has." Margaret Mead

Imagine the possibilities if that group is prayerfully seeking the source of life, truth, meaning and love – the God of the prophets and the Way revealed through Jesus. I pray that our churches will become Quadrant D agents of TRANSFORMATION in the service of God's vision for the reign of justice and righteousness on earth.

ABOUT THE AUTHOR

Trish Towle Greeves, a retired United Church of Christ pastor and former adjunct professor at United Theological Seminary of the Twin Cities, has served churches in Virginia, Minnesota, and Georgia. A graduate of Duke University, she received her M.Div. degree from Virginia Theological Seminary in Alexandria, Virginia and a Doctorate of Ministry degree from United. In addition to *Prophetic Faith* and a personal memoir, she has authored articles in professional journals and co-authored seven Kerygma Bible Study Leader Guides. She currently teaches online courses for the UCC Southeast Conference Pathways Theological Education Program.

An earlier version of this study, *Prophetic Faith: Preparing Your Church to Advocate Social Justice*, was published by Logos Productions in 2010. The copyright contractually reverted to Trish Greeves when Logos ceased operations in 2016.

Made in the USA
Las Vegas, NV
05 September 2023

77116291R00059